Behind Closed Doors

Healing The Emotional Struggless Of South Asians

DR. SHEEZA MOHSIN

Copyright © Sheeza Mohsin, 2020

All rights reserved. No part of this book may be reproduced in any form without permission in writing from the author. Reviewers may quote brief passages in reviews.

Published 2020

DISCLAIMERS

No part of this publication may be reproduced or transmitted in any form or by any means, mechanical or electronic, including photocopying or recording, or by any information storage and retrieval system, or transmitted by email without permission in writing from the author.

Neither the author nor the publisher assumes any responsibility for errors, omissions, or contrary interpretations of the subject matter herein. Any perceived slight of any individual or organization is purely unintentional.

The quotes in this book have been drawn from multiple sources, and are assumed to be accurate in their previously published forms. Every effort has been made to verify both quotes and sources; however, the publisher cannot guarantee their complete accuracy. Brand and product names are trademarks or registered trademarks of their respective owners.

Should you have any concerns regarding material reported, please email the author at sheezacounselor@gmail.com and type EDIT REQUEST in the subject line.

To the coolest dad, Rtn. Abu Mohsin,

Thank you for being my North Star and showing me how to love imperfection.

To Anooshey and Faiz,

Thank you for being my inspiration to be better, work harder, and love wholeheartedly.

To each and every one of you who shared your experience with me, thank you for the honor of choosing me to talk to - as family, as a friend, as your counselor, therapist, and coach.

I am forever grateful

Acknowledgments

I want to begin by saying that behind every successful woman there is an army of supporters, without whom the world cannot be conquered. Mom, I love you and am so grateful for your love. You are my rock. Louis Joachim, I am grateful to have the best father figure I could get in life. You are one of the two people I work hard to make proud. My sisters, Farah and Sehba, your love and unconditional support strengthens my spine. I know everything will be okay because you are there when I'm falling apart.

Anooshey, my daughter and my strength; you have been there for me the way no one could be. Faiz, my son and my energy, you have taught me to love unconditionally, be understanding. Both of you make me proud every day, in living every day the way you do. Asif Dhanani, I will always be grateful for the abundant love you give to our children. Amber Hussain, I now know how it feels to have a sister who grew in my heart. To Afifa and Ali, thank you for loving me with all my flaws. I will always love you and be there for you, no matter what.

Shahid Malik, you are my best friend, always and forever. I will forever be grateful to you for picking me up and watching my back when I have been the most vulnerable. Durriya Shamsi, I have had the pleasure of leaning on you since I was five years old. Your love and compassion makes my life so rich.

Uzma Iqbal, if I ever make something of myself, I will remember the countless times you have told me it's going to happen. Turan Quettawala, thank you for always being there for me. You and Uzma are my safe place. Moneeza Butt, your unconditional love gives me strength and support I cannot explain. Quratulain Adnan, I love you for being there for me at a time in life when I felt very isolated and alone. To all of my friends, all over the Globe: thank you. Life has been rich because of your presence. I will always be grateful.

To Dr. Jennings and Dr. Vittrup, thank you for guiding me and believing in me more than I believed in myself. To all my students and trainees over the years; I have thoroughly enjoyed learning from you. You are the future of a better tomorrow. To all my clients who have given me the honor of sharing their vulnerability with me, thank you. Working with you gave me the courage to put this book together. To Dr. Carol Creech who edited my book with so much love and care, and the Author Incubator team, who nurtured and guided my writing spirit, I thank you from the bottom of my heart.

To Shakeel Rehmane, the first person who suggested I should write a book; I have stories for you when I meet you again up there. To Pappa, my friend and partner in crime; thank you for raising me like you did in a world that didn't approve of it. I miss you every day of my life and will keep working to make you proud. It still hurts a lot that you are gone. This is for you.

Table of Contents

Acknowledgments iv

Foreword 1

    Chapter 1: South Asians And Their Relationships 4

    Chapter 2: What Does Pain Look Like?
    For Us. South Asian Narratives 19

    Chapter 3: Grab A Comfortable Spot,
    Because We Are Going On A Journey 31

Stage One: Uncovering The Uncomfortable 36

    Chapter 4: Introduction To Stage One: Realization
    And Relief 37

    Chapter 5: Assessment Evaluating The Situation
    And Deciding To Get Help 42

    Chapter 6: Uncovering My Story 52

    Chapter 7: Key Concepts For Healthier Relationships 66

    Chapter 8: Confessions And Secrets: Being
    Brave To Reveal And Re-Evaluate 77

Stage Two: Preparing To Change 89

    Chapter 9: Introduction To Stage Two – Preparing To
    Change 90

    Chapter 10: Discovering Why You're Stuck 96

Chapter 11: Forgiveness – Letting Go And Grieving The Loss 108

Chapter 12: Re-Purposing Your Story And Freedom From The Conflict 119

Stage Three: Strengthening ...Always And Forever 131

Chapter 13: Introduction To Stage Three – Strengthen And Thrive 132

Chapter 14: Generating New Goals For Yourself And Your Relationships 138

Chapter 15: Movement Between The Steps And Stages 147

Chapter 16: Managing The Heart's Desire And The Mind's Resistance 152

Chapter 17: Creating A Life Of Healthy Behaviors And Self-Care 163

Chapter 18: What I Wish For You 171

Resources 177

Glossary 181

About The Author 186

Foreword

I want to take this moment to thank you for being curious, wanting to know more, and especially for wanting to learn more about relationships and emotional wellness as it relates to South Asian Culture and people associated with it.

So whether you are someone who is struggling with a relationship, with yourself or starting a new phase in life, my wish for you is to let you know you are not alone. Life is hard and sometimes we just don't have the luxury of choosing how it plays out; our only choice is to respond. Through reading this book, I am hoping you will find clarity when making those choices, and get exposed to terminology and resources to help you have a fulfilling journey moving forward.

This book is designed to help you slow down, and take a moment to sit with your feelings. It is important throughout this journey to be kind to yourself. To forgive yourself for mistakes you may be reflecting on. To grieve all the losses, to heal from the hurt, to forgive when it's so hard; not because the person who hurt you deserves it; but because you must choose to move on. Most importantly, this book is designed to help you to learn how to love abundantly and wholeheartedly; without punishing those who are wanting to love you; because someone else hurt you in the past.

As men and women of South Asian heritage (commonly referred to being 'Desi') we sit with a lot of expectations and even more pride. We are raised to give up pieces of ourselves and what seems important to us, for the sake of our very important relationships. We pride ourselves in compromising and sacrificing, because the other choice feels selfish. My hope for you is that by reading this book, you will start believing that there is a middle ground, where both your desires and the values you were raised with, can co-exist. Make sure to identify a place where you can record your thoughts and feelings as you go through this book. A lot of my clients use their phones to do that... Looking forward to walking with you ...

> "Out beyond ideas of wrongdoing
> and right-doing there is a field.
> I'll meet you there.
> When the soul lies down in that grass
> the world is too full to talk about."
>
> **— Rumi**

DISCLAIMER: Please note that the situations and people described in this book are composites of my professional experience, to protect the privacy of those who have shared their stories with me. Also, the information I share about South Asians does not represent "hard and fast" dictates about the entire population. This is my perspective based on my learning, training and experience.

CHAPTER 1

South Asians And Their Relationships

Ecstatic for a drop is annihilation into the sea, Pain untold of, is remedy on its own.'

— Ghalib

During the initial part of my training as a marriage and family therapist I studied different models of marriages and relationships, and how to improve them. But it didn't matter what the book said - my mind automatically thought in terms of South Asian (*desi*) families, "But what about his mom? What will the in-laws think about this? There is no way coming out would be smooth – it would be a disaster, with or without therapy."

The collective strength of the South Asian family is what draws people to it. The family ties and the celebrations – not to forget the delicious, warm, and savory food – as well as the community coming together are aspects that make this culture beloved and unique. You see this strength when a South Asian person is in the hospital. Family and friends fight over who will bring food to the family of the person who is ill. Hospital waiting rooms have more relatives than healthcare staff. Nurses and physicians take ten seconds to hold their tongues and manage their judgment when they see the hospital room bursting with Indian-smelling food and chai served as if a party is being held.

You see the same affection when a loved one passes away. For weeks, people make the time to come and visit the family that has experienced loss. Temples and mosques host prayers and people are led in prayers for the departed. You see the power of such community during celebrations like Eid, Diwali, Vaisakhi, or Christmas. People come together at homes and places of worship, and you quickly feel that you are not alone, that you belong, and that you have identity and an inclusive community. It motivates young couples to conform to parental expectations and dress their children in ethnic clothes so that they can be loved on and shown off by the grandparents (who can't wait to flaunt their gorgeous, happily married children). Pictures are taken for social media so family and relatives living in their home countries can see the family.

South Asians are commonly considered a *model minority* – that is, a demographic group that is commonly felt in general to be more highly achieving than the overall population. Most of the immigrants in this group are legal, and moved elsewhere for a better life – in particular for the education of their children. They share a strong and anchoring loyalty to family values, which I will talk about in our next chapter. This "model minority" label, held in common with East Asian immigrants requires hard work and deep commitment. Life is good when children go faithfully to Kumon, play chess and tennis, attend Sunday school of their preferred faith, and win spelling bees.

Kids continue in their perfection when they grow into teenagers who are diligent in the faith, have friends who are from the same cultural community, and participate in activities such as robotics, coding, debate, and athletics. It is even better if the boys are in cricket leagues (which are popping up in North America like Starbucks), and the girls learn classical dance or singing. Many of these families then celebrate when children graduate high school as valedictorian or salutatorian, or with admission to an Ivy League school, or a full ride to a well-known college or university. All of these accomplishments trigger dinner and social conversations full of speculation about the future mates they will choose and when the wedding planning can begin.

Life is great when children choose professions in medicine, law, accounting, finance or similar careers, yielding the family as a whole a higher social status. Everything is great when the children marry equally competent and beautiful partners, preferably from the same sub-culture, but definitely from the same faith. Everyone is ecstatic when there is chatter that the son or daughter could be interested in someone, especially if the requirements for a "good family" are met. (This translates into a requirement for a similar social status for girls, and a higher social status for boys, as well as for a similar level of "conservativeness" on the religious and cultural spectrums.)

And then there is even more celebration when the children do finally decide that they are marrying. It gives the aunties and friends endless topics to talk about as a new family is welcomed into their lives. As in Western culture, weddings in South Asian communities are a capstone experience for the entire family, providing the ultimate expression of faith in the future triumphing over the difficulties of the present. Unfortunately, just as in other communities, South Asians can feel isolated when, at temple or *gurdwara*, cultural expectations to have this marvelously happy life feel a bit too overwhelming – perhaps even impossibly out of reach.

Multi-Generation Households

Whether the current generation lives with their South Asian family or not is irrelevant; parental beliefs, preferences, and the pressing need for their wishes to be honored make up a significant part of a typical South Asian household. In North America, it is not uncommon to find a South Asian family with a grandparent living in the house. While this adds a more complex dynamic to the family system, it also enriches family relationships, developing increased respect and love among members in many multi-generational families.

On the flipside, South Asian couples sometimes struggle with managing the balance and boundaries in multigenerational relationships, depending on the overall emotional health of the family. The role of the mother-in-law plays a large part in the power dynamic of the household. In addition, how the grandfather thinks the children should be raised is considered vitally important, even if it is in conflict with the wishes of the parents, due to fear of being considered disrespectful. If the couple starts their marriage with the in-laws witnessing mistakes and observing conflict, then this added chaos can get in the way of strengthening the new relationship (especially if the parents are not respectful of the couple's boundaries in the first place). In severe cases, this disruptive role of the in-laws is known to be an extreme stressor in the dynamics of a couple's relationship. Issues can range from as small as how the kitchen should be managed, to as large as having a mother-in-law generating feelings of guilt if more attention, time, or money are spent on the wife. Interference in how the couple handles their parenting roles can put a strain on marital relationships as well.

Religion and Culture

The elements of religion and culture contribute to a special dance that each South Asian family expresses uniquely. In addition, the way that each family performs this dance takes precedence over all other ways of practice. This dance shows up frequently as a conflict over marriage and child-rearing decisions, among others. While more progressive families of South Asian heritage can show a great deal of grace and acceptance to variations of this dance within the family system, many other families struggle with feelings of guilt and shame. These feelings center around concerns about abandoning their faith and culture as they grow in their new, bi-cultural identity. Needless to say, the husband's parents' wishes have privilege over the wife's parents in most cases. The exceptions to this rule usually only occur when the wife's family has a higher level of financial affluence or social standing.

For example, if the parents are moderate-to-conservative and the children are liberal, many couples develop a secret life, with certain parts of their relationship concealed. For a dating couple, this could mean that they will not share with their parents that they are sexually intimate. Or if a couple drinks socially, which is taboo behavior, it will not be shared with their parents. The same goes for the social preferences of these children before they marry. Dressing conservatively is expected from the girls, and so they will have more revealing wardrobes, concealed from their parents, which are reserved for their social lives.

Social media has not been helpful in keeping these secrets safe! So many times, the secret lives get revealed and parents or spouses find out one way or the other, that there is another side of life their child identifies with, which they were not aware of. At any given time in our lives, most of us are trying to live and be, without offending or hurting or even disrespecting another person or relationship that is important to us. Social media has also altered the expectations in relationships to a large degree. Every so often I hear about hurt feelings because a loved one or friend did not 'like' a post or did not post something significantly deep on someone's wall. For other apps that send 'streaks', the unopened ones communicate rejection and make the person sending it so vulnerable. Text messages feel strange if not answered while private stories and fake accounts can control who gets to see the 'real' person.

Another element of that struggle includes interaction with the family's faith community. Going to places of worship and being eyed by the "aunties," whose children have tattled on the liberal children and shown the "disgraceful" pictures of them on social media, can eventually become a source of isolation from the community. Additionally, choosing religious education for children becomes tricky if you live a liberal lifestyle. While many parents still feel that religious education is valuable, the fear of judgment within their faith community may keep them away from participating.

Family and Social Pressure

Due to the high level of interaction that South Asian families have with each other, this culture is not well-known for respecting personal boundaries. What relatives, family friends, or the larger community will think about a child's actions plays a huge role in controlling decisions taken within the family. For example, if a girl wants to marry outside of a community, even though the family has interacted with the boy and seems to find that he meets most of their criteria for a successful match, they may be inclined to say no. The family considers the domineering relative who would be against the marriage, or about how much shame was brought upon another person in their social group who did something similar – and so they wind up disagreeing with it completely.

Male Privilege

Even though male privilege is a global reality, it can present especially strongly in the South Asian community. Regardless of whether a boy is raised in India, Pakistan, Bangladesh, or by people with that heritage across the Atlantic, male privilege is quickly realized by South Asian children growing up. It is obvious back home, where girls are not allowed to go to school and boys are. It is obvious in North America, when some girls are not allowed to participate in sports simply because of the clothing they are supposed to wear, or because it will entail trips away from home for tournaments.

Male privilege again shows up back home when the son's professional pursuit is financially supported, but the cultural value that the daughter is *paraai* (she will eventually "belong" to her husband and his family) gets in the way of financial support for her education. It shows up in North America when a daughter is told she must pursue college locally, but the son can leave home to go live in the dorms. Much of this is done to protect the family's honor, in the form of the girl's virginity or reputation; if she is seen socializing with boys and men, she will lose value in the eyes of the community. The dance can become deadly if a daughter wants to marry outside her community or faith and it is completely forbidden. She may even be sacrificed in the form of an honor killing, or ousted from her home for choosing to dishonor her family in such a way. Elements of male privilege continue to seep into South Asian women's lives even as they pursue robust careers, make their own money, and begin to thrive. Many of them have to manage feelings of shame and guilt for wanting something for themselves, or about leaving their children for work or travel, or about having their husbands working inside the home to help out around the house.

Class, Socioeconomic Status, and Education

As in any culture or community, many of the challenges and privileges found in the South Asian community are anchored in socio-economic status (SES) and privilege. Financial class, education level, and social standing (both at home and in North America) influence the unsaid rules set by South Asian society that certain expectations will be followed.

For lower SES groups, the pressure to follow religious and cultural norms is even stronger than it is for those of a higher SES level. 'Gender bias' and 'male privilege' within family systems also increase as education level goes down, regardless of financial status.

Marriage

Working primarily as a couple's therapist, I am most fascinated by the South Asian model of marriage, and what the common threads are that anchor the idea of "a good marriage" for my clients. There are some key elements that make up this model of marriage, and which may seem a bit different from the Western marriage model.

For one thing, I notice the extreme importance of the acceptance level (or resistance level) of the husband's parents and family toward girls entering the family. This includes the attitudes of key family members toward the newcomer: parents, sisters, older siblings, and even favorite children. Other key elements of the South Asian marriage model are the need to build trust and credibility with the in-laws early on in the marriage. People walking into the relationship are quite aware of this dynamic; barring folks outside the culture. In addition, boundaries set by the husband (or the lack of them) are absolutely vital when it comes to how much interference or influence his family will be allowed to have on the couple's relationship. You may wonder why I have not mentioned the actual marriage itself – this is deliberate for several reasons. First, all of these power dynamics (or "pain points") continue to play a role in the marriage over time, and can add to the resentment or challenges within other relationships. Secondly the dynamic of the couple's relationship is influenced greatly by whether they live with in-laws and other family members or are living separately. Thirdly, conflicts within a couple can be magnified when living with family and or when family visits them. Finally, the expectation greatly falls on the wife to do justice to honor her husbands' family and to show her commitment to the family, while the same is not expected from the husband with regard to his in-laws.

The Stereotypical South Asian Marriage

There are five key elements of most stereotypical, desi marriage, in my view:

1. The man is the head of the household and manages the money, regardless of who generates the income.

2. Similar to most cultures, the woman is responsible for food and home management, as well being the primary responsible party for parenting. This is true regardless of whether or not she works outside the home.

3. The weight of making the relationship successful generally lies more on the wife's shoulder's as she is socialized to believe she must sacrifice her needs for the family.

4. The husband chooses how financial decisions are executed in the family, and in most cases, handles all financial matters.

5. Intimacy needs of the husband take precedence over intimacy needs of the wife.

Sexuality

The South Asian view of sexual expression is generally conservative, and sexual curiosity and/or exploration is a taboo topic with a strong stigma surrounding it. Sex is often considered something dirty or shameful, if talked about outside of wanting children. Sexual assertiveness is not encouraged in women. Women may land in my office crying profusely about feeling inadequate when their husband or partner is no longer sexually "chasing" them. The shame of having a higher sexual libido makes them feel isolated from their friends, who, in contrast, seem to be sick of constantly having to "put out" in their own relationships. Men struggle with their sexual expression as they experience erectile dysfunction or testosterone deficiency due to various medical and emotional challenges. They have even more limited options to seek help. The stigma around going to get counseling does not help the situation either.

In general, there seems to be a widely held view in South Asian culture that men have the privilege to express their own sexual curiosity, whether it involves trying anal sex or watching pornography. These are not activities that a "regular" desi woman can explore on her own without meeting a significant amount of judgment.

Divorce – and what comes with it

Divorce rates among desi communities in North America may be higher than they are at home, but nevertheless divorce is still considered very unfavorably, and most South Asians do not prefer to exit a relationship. As a result, the "miserable marriage" rate for the South Asian community is; high. The stigma of divorce is still great, and it carries with it associations of failure, shame, and the impression of being somehow broken or damaged.

This situation has begun to change over the past decade, and it has been heartening to see that many South Asian families are able to experience divorce with strength and grace. Learning to evolve from the experience has resulted in the creation of more resilient children post-divorce. One huge reason for this change is the rise of better educated and more economically independent mothers, who are able to continue providing a stable and consistent life to their children no matter what their marital status may be.

Marriage outside the culture

We hear a strong loyalty to marrying within the culture, especially within the faith. In addition, while many parents are now aware that their children are using dating apps in order to find someone special in their lives, there still may be a subtle, implied criticism that many people can hear when sharing that they met using an app. South Asian children also feel the shame of betrayal if they abandon their faith. There is shame in marrying the "other," whether in terms of race, ethnicity, and religion.

People of South Asian descent who have chosen life partners from another culture can have various struggles interacting with their home culture. I have heard this from both clients and others, and I see that this is also; a unique dance of sorts. It's as if choosing your life comes at the cost of feeling sidelined by your own culture and community. Multi-cultural couples can benefit from many elements of adjusting to life in their host culture, viewing their experiences as both enriching and fulfilling. Nevertheless, their own cultural connections to home may suffer significantly.

Some of the challenges experienced by partners of South Asians include language barriers, and consequently feeling excluded when socializing with family and community. The key challenge that many children face, especially in families with limited English skill, is a resulting isolation from parents, who don't speak the other language. The parents can feel a sense of being betrayed by their children, when the grandchildren cannot speak the home language. This is especially true with regard to their sons, who appear to be preferring a new culture and way of life over the way they were raised. Living with that guilt is hard for many sons and daughters. This guilt becomes isolating, as they cannot express the sense of loss they feel when they cannot share aspects of their culture with their spouse, or aspects of the culture that they miss.

I know reading the above may give you a feeling of heaviness, given that I have presented so many of the complicated elements of our community. Know that the goal is for you to realize you are not the only one and help is right around the corner, in another chapter. As your guide through this journey I want to emphasize the importance of understanding, so that you don't just treat your symptoms; you treat the root of the problem. Rest assured this is the ground work needed to prepare you for the healing that is to come. The steps identified in later chapters will help relieve so much of the conflict inside of yourself, so that you can pursue your happiness and joy. I have walked in your path, and failed before I "got it". I am confident you will get there too. The goals you set in your journey could redefine your life and how you live it, forever.

CHAPTER 2

What Does Pain Look Like? For Us. South Asian Narratives

'Therapy Is Different When Your Therapist Has Walked in some of your truth.'

One of the main reasons I wrote this book was to send out a message to as many people as possible who have South Asian roots (specifically from India, Pakistan, and Bangladesh). My message is that that they are not alone, or weird, or not good enough, in the struggles they are experiencing with their marriage, family, or life in general. While our culture is rich in heritage, beautiful traditions, and ritual, it is also entrenched in judgments, criticism, and unreasonable expectations of perfection, especially for those who may have any kind of social, economic, or racial privilege. The old saying that "Much is expected from those who are given much" is very true in desi culture.

Essentially, this privilege I talk about could be any privilege. For example, when one is a parent, they have a privilege if they live in North America (or anywhere outside the home country). Or someone may have the privilege of being intelligent, or of showing some kind of potential or talent. And then, as the result of having said talent, for example, one deals with the fact that the family has a "mission" to make them into a masterpiece, so that they can be proud of them.

Now, before I start presenting what may be seen as criticism of some South Asian values, please understand that there are many desi individuals out there who live healthy, balanced lives in a wholehearted way, as Brené Brown would say. (Brené is a noted University of Houston research professor who holds an endowed chair in the field of social work. She studies the emotions of shame, empathy, and courage in human social interactions.)

Nevertheless, my clients of South Asian heritage have many common issues. If you are reading this as a person of South Asian heritage, and you are trying to understand your family, your husband, your wife, or simply to understand the way you, yourself, think, then this book is for you! In my experience, most individuals who identify as being connected to a South Asian heritage appear to have a strong loyalty to traditional beliefs and values that may or may not serve them well in their current life situation. I can help you sort these issues out in this book.

What you are about to read are statements of intensity, experienced by those from our culture. Please note that there are so many issues that individuals, couples and families experience that I couldn't possibly include them all here. My wish for you here is for you to feel heard, supported and possibly relieved to know that if you have felt this way, there are so many others who have as well. The groups included here, expressing their pain, are representing topics that I have seen a lot of in the desi community. This is a limited list, but will give you an idea of some common struggles experienced by the community. See if these comments speak your truth, as well.

The challenges of Teenagers..

"I am getting tired. I am so sick of the hypocrisy. Why did they even move here if they like the values back home? I'm sure it would have been easier back home."

"People from good families don't date. They only marry. How does that even make sense? How am I supposed to know someone is good for me unless I spend time with them?"

"I'm gay and I will never be able to come out to my parents. I hope they realize that it helps me feel numb – that is why I'm cutting. It makes the curse of who I am feel less painful."

"If someone sees you with a boy, they assume you are sleeping with him. Really? Mom and Dad, not every boy I talk to is interesting in marrying me! We are friends and we go to

the same school – why are you making basic life so complicated for me? Let me feel normal."

"I can't study with her because her body is too developed, and I have to find boys to study with? I can't believe my parents said that."

"I am just asking them to let me go to the movies. My parents say, 'Sure you can go out with him to the movies. I'll come too and sit far away so I can keep an eye on you.' Are you kidding me!?"

"I have depression. My parents tell me it's because my faith is weak. I should pray more."

"I love her. She's not from our culture. She understands me more than anyone ever has but my dad threatened to remove me from his will if I date her."

Marriage & Sexuality

"I am frustrated but I can't share that. They love her. She is so bubbly and friendly when she is at a gathering of friends or when we are hosting. It is after that, when that I find out whose husband bought their wives what and took their vacation where, and that we should do that too. Not to mention making me feel like she married below her level and could have been so much better off if she married someone with more money. I am tired of feeding her insecurity. The clothes and the shopping is too much when we should be *saving. I feel so frustrated. I don't want to go near her. I'm tired of this rut we are in."*

"How do I even tell my mom I crave a sexual connection and we have not been intimate for years? Yes, years. It is so hard for me to stay composed when my friends talk about their husbands not getting enough. It makes me feel less-than. My body feels abandoned. I feel alone. I crave for him to just hold me in his arms, or kiss me or just lay next to me, focused on me. Is that too unreasonable. I feel hopeless and sad."

"I never realized having an intellectual connection would be so important. We have nothing to talk about other than the kids. It gives me a feeling of emptiness. We cannot discuss current affairs, or political issues or even argue for the sake of argument. I desire that so much."

"When she rejects sexual intimacy I wonder if it is because she doesn't find me attractive or if she doesn't love me. It hurts as that is the primary way I know how to show emotions. Just because we argued doesn't mean we don't have to be intimate. I am shutting down because if I say something she doesn't like she will not have sex with me. I think it is unfair. I get so angry thinking about it."

"I was raised here. I speak this language. Yes I speak Hindi too but our way of communicating is so different. Her responses are so uncouth and everything is about pleasing her family or my family. What about me? It seems like a show we

have to put on. I want to go on a date with her and she always wants to do something with the family. What about us? She constantly dismisses me until she gets confirmation from a family member that they agree with what I said. I feel so emotionally disconnected from her."

"Yes I am one of the unfortunate ones who makes more money than her husband. Managing his esteem and insecurities is the full time job I didn't see coming. What hurts the most is that he will still find something to criticize me on, and dump everything else on me too. Is this what a single mom feels like? Anything he does around the house seems like a favor for me. Every effort is made not to help, but to put me down and shame me in some way. I feel alone. It is so hard. When my kids see him yelling at me, I see the fear in their eyes. This is my life, and it will never change."

Infidelity

"This is the third time I've caught him with her. He begs me to stay and says that it will never happen again. I fall for it. Then it happens again. I don't know why I'm staying in this relationship. I am so ashamed of staying in this relationship. I know I have to, or my home will break. Its not the kids' fault and they will suffer so much."

"She says I made her feel inadequate and he makes her feel wonderful. She's the mother of my children. Does she think

it's been easy for me to stay with her? I never crossed that line and God knows I could have. I feel hopeless."

"He says he loves her. That she is willing to accept me. He says he won't leave me but doesn't love me anymore."

"How could she be so selfish? She says it was a mistake. How do you make a mistake like this?"

Divorce

'They tell me to stay with him. That it would be a source of shame. That is why they say girls should not be educated too much. Once they become independent they don't want to listen to their husbands.'

"I want to leave. I am tired of pleasing him. Tired of being criticized every day. I am done.'

'I don't feel like coming home to her. I try to make excuses so I don't go home early. I avoid her. I don't want to touch her. I want to leave. This is it."

"Why should I stay? To show to the world we are married so we can continue to be invited to parties? I will be responsible for my kids regardless. I'm done pretending I'm happy. I want to be really happy."

Aging Parents and Protocol

"I don't like to see them fight about my care. Never thought I'd be so dependent on them. I wish I never left home."

"It hurts me when all that matters are his parents. Mine can be sick or needing me but I need to care for his parents and have been doing that for so long. Then to hear those painful words, "tum karti kya ho" (what do you do for them?) is hurtful and resentful. How am I supposed to be excited when he then wants to have sex?"

Childhood Tragedies: Incest, Sexual Abuse

"I was molested by my grandfather. Who does that? For years, before I was brave and old enough to tell mom, I stayed silent. When Mom stays loyal to him and shuts me up, I hate her."

"He was teaching religion and prayers. The first time I thought he was being loving. I was an eight-year-old boy. He was an older cousin. He told me I would like it too. He was a jerk."

"He was my uncle and acting so loving toward my dad. He brought the best presents and told me it was our secret. Every time my husband comes near me, I think of that nasty man. I feel miserable and raped. I think my husband wants to leave me because I can't be sexual with him."

"She was considered a member of the family. She told me we were playing bride and groom and that was how the game went. I was the groom, so I had to touch her there. I get angry and only like sex when I'm in control. My wife thinks I'm rough. How can I tell her about this? She is still alive, and we have to see her when we go home."

"My brother – he is my brother and I felt unsafe always. Mom told me to not tell Dad. What was wrong with her?"

Mental Health, Learning and Mood Disorders

"When the doctors said she had bi-polar disorder, they broke off the engagement. She is doing so well on the medicine. He seemed like such a sweet boy, but in the first blink of adversity he left her because his parents said 'no'. Maybe this is best for her."

"They know he is on the spectrum, but they insist on asking me when he will start college. Is this a joke? I have never felt so isolated and alone as I have sometimes when struggling with his diagnosis."

"Her mother-in-law said she is lazy. She says she is irresponsible and is just busy on Facebook. Her husband accused her of being crazy because she got carried away with shopping so much. We did not know what ADD was. I feel so bad for my daughter. We just thought she was not smart enough for college."

"It's a Jin (spirit) inside her. Then we pray and its gone. It's in our religion. The doctor thinks psychotropic medicine will help. We just stopped them because she got worse."

"He is so productive and works so hard for weeks. I think he doesn't even sleep then. Then there comes a time when he starts feeling low. His feet can barely drag him into the bathroom."

Domestic Violence

"I know he loves me. It's just that sometimes he can't control his temper. It isn't that bad all the time. When he pushed me down the stairs, we were arguing close to them or I wouldn't have fallen so hard."

"She is my daughter. I'm seventy-eight and physically dependent on her. When she hit me the last time, my grandson called the police. I denied it. I understand her frustration."

Remarriage

"I crave connection. I want someone I can romance every day. I want to love on her like no one has loved her before. I know she's good for me. Then all the heartache from the past floods my mind – to let someone in and feel the pain I felt. I need to protect myself. It's not worth it. They are all the same. I will not make a fool out of myself again."

"He says so many negative things to me. I hate it when he adds, 'This is why your husband must have left you.' It jabs my heart with a knife. If I leave, my parents will feel so much shame. I have to just live with him even though I die every day."

"I am tired. I play so many roles, I feel like I am a machine that will run out of battery any day. I have to be responsible – the perfect "everything" for everyone. I need to be a perfect mom for my kids, a perfect daughter for my parents, a perfect daughter-in-law, and the list goes on.

"I just want to be loved by him, for him to notice me. I want to be romanced and feel passion and wanted. I want him to whisper in my ear so it can send goose bumps down my spine. I want him to put his arm around me when we are out with friends and kiss my forehead or cheek in front of others. I want him to compliment me in front of others. I seek his validation."

I understand that this may have been hard to read, and even more difficult if some of this is similar to what is going on with you. Feelings are big and when they felt deeply it is so difficult to push them out completely. It puts us in this helpless state of mind where we feel like either running away from the situation or end up dealing with it with such strong emotion that it becomes even more destructive. The worst is when we do nothing at all, but silently suffer and let these feelings eat us from the inside.

I am happy to tell you that relief is on the way. In the next chapter I will talk about how to read the rest of the book so you can take a deep dive into your life and learn about yourself and your relationships. It is when you start untangling and organizing those thoughts and challenges that you will be closer to the root of the major elements of life that are getting in your way of being your best self. That is when you will start feeling empowered to learn, grow and thrive. So be kind to yourself as you figure out what baby steps you need to take to start this journey.

'You yourself, as much as anyone in the entire universe, deserves your love and affection.'

— Buddha

CHAPTER 3

Grab A Comfortable Spot, Because We Are Going On A Journey

"Why do I talk about the benefits of failure?

Simply because failure meant a stripping away of the inessential. I stopped pretending to myself that I was anything other than what I was, and began to direct all my energy into finishing the only work that mattered to me."

— **J.K. Rowling**

How this Book Is Organized

It is very important as you embark on this journey that you think about what made you want to read this book. What is making you curious about learning more about you, your marriage or your romantic relationships, or your family? Why now and why not earlier? What are you struggling with? What do your desire to change in your life so you feel fulfilled? Is it just one thing or many? These are important questions for consideration.

My goal for writing this book is not just to introduce you to certain concepts, so you can start understanding yourself as well as the relationships surrounding you, but to tell you I have failed a lot, and then some. Working on myself and learning from my work has helped me, as I continue to work through my challenges. I am sharing some key learnings for you to start your journey toward healing. The key term here is 'start'. This book as barely a hundred plus some pages for a reason: it will pave the way for you to organize your thoughts and understanding about why you are the way you are and why you struggle the way you do. It will not solve everything, but it will kick start the journey.

The first two chapters have been focused on helping you see that your journey may look unique but actually has so much in common with the struggles of others. You will find many quotes of feelings or narratives, so that you can understand their overall perspective and find the similarity between your experiences.

The beginning of Chapter four is where your therapeutic journey of discovery, insight, and possible healing begins. You will learn how to reframe elements of yourself and your relationships in terminology that may help you gain a deeper understanding. Remember, many of the concepts I introduce may be new to you, so feel free to search them online if any of them spark your interest in knowing more. You will see that the coming chapters are arranged as three sets (or blocks) of four chapters each. Each of the three blocks will focus on the three different stages of the insight-filled journey that you are about to take. I'm excited for you and to be walking with you.

Stage One

Stage one is where I focus on helping you uncover your history and seeing where you have been. Concepts such as your *genogram*, family history, and loyalties are revealed. Your relationship with your parents and siblings will be discussed in order to help you understand the major influences of your life. These chapters educate you about relationship elements generally uncovered in therapy or counseling, and I will discuss concepts such as *attachment* and *codependence* within a South Asian framework. How your sub-culture presents in North America (which depends on your family's socio-economics, immigration status, and history) is also explored so that you can begin to understand any privilege or adversity you may have experienced. You may find you are starting to be honest and clear about the problem, or problems, that burdens you - either as the secret you have never shared or as the heavy baggage you carry with you every day. Whether you are concerned about a strained relationship, marital infidelity, sexual orientation issue, or mental illness (such as depression), this chapter may give you the courage to recognize your truth and acknowledge it.

Stage Two

Stage two gives you a deeper understanding of why you have not been able to resolve your challenges, and begin to learn the possible interactions of individual and family dynamics that may have gotten in your way. These chapters discuss concepts that you will need to understand in order to get clarity regarding the dynamic in which your problems are entangled. My goal is to prime your mind to create a clear vision of what you want to change in your life. Here you will also find a focus on honoring your past and grieving the losses you have experienced.

Stage Three

The chapters that introduce stage three, equip you with critical information and techniques needed to mobilize your plan to initiate change; it also aids you in identifying the resources you will need to help you through this change. These chapters also expose you to some basic techniques and tips to help you create better goals and plans so that you can more easily identify what needs to change in your life and do something about it. You will also be exposed to tools you can use for self-care both now and in the future.

The last few chapters will explain the challenges you may face as you start attempting to implement and sustain these changes in your life. As experts say that life will keep 'life-ing' at you (Angela Laurea) while you are attempting change. Your focus should be on creating a space to change along with your adventures and limitations. I also spend time explaining the cycle of change and resistance so that you can understand why you are hitting roadblocks even as you work to implement change.

A moment of reflection...

I have seen many of my clients, colleagues, friends and family members experience challenges and struggles while feeling helpless and hopeless. More importantly, I have been there myself. The pain, the isolation, and the shame (to name a few emotions) are all too familiar. I want to remind you again to be kind to yourself. You have come this far and attempted your best solution with the skills, resources and circumstances life presented. An expert had said that you cannot solve a problem you may have created, at the same level of intelligence you have created it. You need to grow and rise so you can look at it with a stronger and deeper lens. I have an idea of what you may have experienced, and I will be here as your guide throughout this exciting journey towards healing and strengthening. Things <u>can</u> get better I know. Let's begin!

STAGE ONE

Uncovering The Uncomfortable

CHAPTER 4

Introduction To Stage One: Realization And Relief

What can you expect in stage one? This is your first deep dive into making sense of your life and the journey you are on. This block of chapters is where you can find concepts, terminology, and stories that may help you understand why you are the way you are. Just below is a summary of what we are going to cover.

You will begin with an assessment to understand if you should consider working with a professional up front versus going through this book. This is an important decision as this book is by no means a replacement for professional help, which some of you may benefit from.

After the assessment you will begin to explore your heritage and your family history, which is the foundation of your story. Understanding your family background and immigration history can be a therapeutic experience. This is why you love, fight, and connect in a certain way. Your brothers and sisters and your family's overall emigration narrative contribute to your rich bi-cultural identity.

You will further explore the culture and values that belong to your family, and to the surrounding community with which your family prefers to associate. You will understand what it means to have roots in a *collective culture,* even while you are raised in, or spend your life in, an *individualistic culture.* You will make sense of why your family emphasizes certain values which may not make sense to you. You will also get an introduction to terms, like *codependence*, within a cultural context and boundaries, so that you can more easily grasp what it means to be in codependent relationships. You may get an idea of why your family enjoys certain privileges, and yet does not benefit from some of the social freedoms that are available to other people in North America.

What Will Help You

It will be helpful for you to start a journal for your journey. Many of my clients, especially men, keep this journal on their phone. For every topic and chapter that you read, label it with the heading and briefly write down what is in that chapter that uniquely applies to you and your family. In this way, when you work with a therapist (either with me or someone else), you will have already organized many of your thoughts into categories. This makes the process of exploring your issues more effective.

What May Get in Your Way?

Remember that the deep dive can only be as deep as you are ready to handle. Sometimes that may only be a few feet, and that is okay. Be kind to yourself as you go through this process. There may be a lot of thoughts that surface, and you may or may not be able to make sense of them all. I caution you not to engage in *minimizing* or *glorifying*, which are terms that I will explain just below.

Minimizing

When you *minimize*, you don't give as much empathy, compassion or understanding to an emotion, event, or occurrence as it probably deserves. For example, saying, "I was raped only once, and I was only twelve years old. It was so long ago, and it never happened again because I told my mother about it." Rape is a serious physical, mental, and emotional violation, and its impact can be severe. It is important for you to grieve the experience and sit with those emotions in order to truly process what happened. Minimizing helps you to distract yourself from the pain whenever you recall this event, but in the long-term minimizing prevents you from really coming to terms with a traumatic event.

Glorifying

In contrast, when you *glorify* something, you report things as being better than they really are/were. You might say, "I had such a nice, safe childhood. My parents worked, so we didn't see them much, but they loved us and provided so well for us. I am so grateful for them. My younger sister and I pretty much took care of ourselves. I loved playing mommy." However, this doesn't really sound like as great a situation as it is being described. Being raised as a latchkey kid in North America can be intimidating for many people, and unfortunately many immigrant children have no choice but to be left at home to take care of themselves until their parents get home. Once they become adults these individuals may be able to minimize their past issues with sitters and adult caregivers, but a certain amount of emotional support may have been lacking in their lives growing up. This situation may have taken a toll on the emotional development of such adult children, and this fact needs to be acknowledged and understood.

Reminder about Self-Care

During this process, it's important to be kind to yourself. Don't do all of these activities totally by yourself or at a high rate of speed. Journaling your feelings two to three times a week is more than enough. Daily journaling or processing may leave you emotionally fatigued, and not in the best emotional frame of mind. If you feel more depressed than usual, please make an appointment with a counselor who can help you deal with the issues that have come up for you.

Now, I invite you to get ready to take a deep dive into reflecting on where you have been and where you are in your life as you take this bold step to self-discovery.

CHAPTER 5

Assessment Evaluating The Situation And Deciding To Get Help

―――――○―――――

"Beyond the earth, beyond the farthest skies, I try to find Heaven and Hell. Then I hear a solemn voice that says: "Heaven and hell are inside."

— Omar Khayyam, the Rubaiyat of Omar Khayyam

You've thought through a lot of your history, trauma, and challenges, and this chapter will help you assess the level of expertise you may need to assist you. I want to make it clear that this book is no replacement for a mental health professional working with you; it is important for you to seek professional help if it is warranted.

For most individuals, and not just South Asians, the idea of getting help has a lot of stigma attached to it. Growing up, most of us hear needing 'help' as a sign of weakness, failure and defeat so much that we would rather suffer in silence than express the reality of what we may be experiencing. Let me begin by telling you a few things to consider as you are acknowledging your feelings and your mental health. Here is a modified list from what the American Psychological Association suggests you consider to determine if you need to seek professional help. If you are experiencing a few of these, it is important to consider seeking a Mental Health professional:

Severe Symptoms:

- Suicidal Thoughts / Ideation
- Multiple health challenges
- Difficulty in completing daily activities such as going to school, taking care of children, or going to work.
- Severe anger and physical harm toward self or others
- Self-harm such as cutting.
- Excessive crying

Moderate Symptoms:

- Feeling fatigue such that you are sleeping a lot more than usual
- Eating a lot or very little
- Having little empathy for anyone
- Excessive worrying
- Feeling hopeless and not enjoying doing things you typically enjoy doing
- Feeling anxiety constantly

Mild Symptoms:

- Social withdrawal
- Getting impatient with important relationships
- Feeling resentment
- Feeling overwhelmed and that you cannot manage all that is on your plate
- Not being able to focus on tasks that need to be completed

Remember, our mind is one of the most valuable organs in our body, and also probably the most ignored. It is important to make sure that you have some clarity on the level of care you need. As you start thinking about the goals you would like to work on, I invite you to consider an overall wellness check. While there are many versions of it, a wellness check may help you look at your overall well-being. Given that most of us are a work in progress, it is important for you to identify which part of your life needs attention first. In this section, I will list elements of your wellness that you may want to pay attention to.

Emotional Wellness

- Elements that present emotional wellness include:
- Feeling content most of the time

- Being able to talk to others about your emotional challenges
- Saying no when you need to
- Having a healthy community for support
- Feeling good about yourself

Challenges to emotional wellness that need to be tended to include:

- Stress
- Sleep
- Mental health
- Lack of work/ Life balance

I notice for many of my clients that emotional health and overall stress are often ignored, especially for busy professionals and executives. It is hard for us to report, or recognize, that we cannot handle some things.

Environmental Wellness

- Being aware of the limits of the earth's natural resources
- Conserving energy (i.e. shutting off unused lights)
- Recycling paper, cans, and glass as much as possible
- Enjoying and appreciating time outside in natural settings

- Not polluting the air, water, or earth (planting trees and having a lower carbon footprint as examples)
- Creating home and work environments that are supportive and nurturing

Living in a clean and organized space to being and responsible for your neighborhood or community gives you a sense of responsible citizenship that has compounding positive impact, on both you and your environment.

Financial Wellness

- Learning how to manage your money and establishing a personal budget
- Not living beyond your means
- Making a plan to pay back your student loans
- Learning about debt and how to manage it
- Building good credit
- Thinking long term (i.e. setting up a savings account)
- Learning not to let money be the driving force of your life
- Donating some of your money, if possible, to a cause you believe in

This is probably one of the most real stresses that I see clients impacted with, outside of emotional health. Many desi families and couples can fall into the trap of spending more than their means, and living a lifestyle of debt. The pressures of social media and comparing one's life with others does not help. Many families as a result; choose to save a minimal amount and spend in anticipation of income. The level of anxiety and hopelessness that comes with the challenge of financial distress is intense. Working with a financial counselor is a good decision to start getting financially healthy.

Intellectual Wellness

- Being able to challenge yourself to see all sides of an issue
- Becoming a critical thinker
- Developing your own ideas, views, and opinions
- Exposing yourself to new ideas, people, and beliefs that are different from your own
- Becoming aware of who you are and what you value

I have noticed that my clients who read articles and continuously gain knowledge and learning, do extremely well in therapy. Their brain is continuously exposed to new information and stays sharp and malleable.

Occupational Wellness

- Doing work that you find motivating and interesting

- Understanding how to balance leisure with work
- Working in a way that fits into your personal learning style
- Communicating and collaborating with others
- Working independently and with others
- Feeling inspired and challenged
- Feeling good at the end of the day about the work you accomplished

Given that we spend most of our waking hours working, whether we work inside the home or outside, it is critical that we find it motivating, meaningful and interesting. Having a feeling of accomplishment is imperative to your overall satisfaction with life in general. As an example, moms who take a lot of pride in taking care of their home and find meaning and joy in raising kids, have a healthier self-esteem than those who may focus on the fatigue (which is very real) and being overwhelmed in general.

Social Wellness

- Developing assertive skills, not passive or aggressive ones
- Balancing social and personal time
- Being yourself in all situations

- Becoming engaged with other people in your community
- Valuing diversity and treating others with respect
- Continually being able to maintain and develop friendships and social networks
- Creating boundaries within relationships that encourage communication, trust, and conflict management
- Remembering to have fun
- Having a supportive network of family and friends
- Nurturing a healthy marriage and/or healthy romantic relationship

Given that the desi community is more socially inclined, I notice many clients experience stress and anxiety in social situations. Not having healthy boundaries, and doing things for others at the cost of negatively impacting yourself and your important relationships, is a common symptom I notice when working with South Asian clients.

Spiritual Wellness

- Developing a purpose in life
- Having the ability to spend reflective time alone
- Having the ability to explain why you believe what you believe, and what is right and wrong

- Caring and acting for the welfare of others and the environment
- Being able to practice forgiveness and compassion in life
- Practicing spirituality through faith, labyrinths, mandalas, meditation, yoga, or prayer

This seems to be a more evolved area for the desi community. While most people are anchored to their religion, there are those who may not be following the conventional faiths of this region, such as Hinduism, Islam, Christianity and Sikhism, Buddhism, Baha'ism to name a few; some do believe in being Agnostic or Atheist in their beliefs. It is then hard for families to relate to and understand this position. This may induce isolation and alienation from the community. Please be aware of your own sense of Spirituality so you can feel whole and content. If there is a struggle, it is important to reach out for help.=

Overall Physical Health

- Dental health
- Physical activities
- Energy level
- Physical fitness (can you climb stairs without losing your breath)

- Sexual health
- Hospitalizations and Emergency room visits in the past 3-6 months

While this book is focused more on relationships and emotional/psychological health, I want to make sure you are paying attention to your physical health and any symptoms that may need more attention. It is important to get an annual physical exam at the least and the recommended set of exams and tests you need, based on your health, age and genetics. This is even more important if you are a smoker, consume alcohol, drugs or take medications for health conditions.

It is important that you take a look at your overall health and identify key areas that you need to pay attention to. Be as authentic and transparent as you possibly can.

(Source: University of New Hampshire. Health and Wellness. Wellness Wheel)

CHAPTER 6

Uncovering My Story

"...when you have lived my life, then you can judge me."
— **Anonymous**

When you start working on personal issues, the first step is to take a look at how you got where you are now. Your heritage, upbringing, genetic makeup, past and present relationships, and indeed the very reason why you decided to pursue self-discovery or counseling now, as opposed to at any prior time, are all important to notice. Let's start with a few critical elements of this self-discovery.

Your Heritage

An important element of why you are the way you are is due to the culture, traditions, and legacy of the individuals in your extended family. These factors profoundly influence how your mind is hard-wired, and how you make sense of what is right, wrong, good, and terrible. Socio-economic status is an example of your heritage. Your ancestors' lives in the affluent (or not so affluent) areas of Dacca, Delhi, or Islamabad will impact the kinds of homes, neighborhoods, and material goods you prefer over others. Perhaps you may come from a middle-class family that worked their way up to where they are now in life. Perhaps everyone in your family worked hard and lived within their means, so that even when you are doing well financially, your feel wrong or frivolous spending money on more luxurious items. This type of emotional heritage is no less real than when your genetic makeup makes you more vulnerable to heart disease or diabetes. These behaviors and practices can be explained as family loyalties, and will be discussed next.

Identify Your Family Loyalties

Families can owe their loyalty to many things. Family loyalties can include behaviors, practices, rituals, and even preferences that have been ingrained into the social and emotional fabric of a family's relationships. Many of these loyalties are quite beneficial. They could be healthy activities, such as everyone in the family liking to workout, or play outdoors; perhaps the men in the family play cricket or golf. They could be rituals, such as getting together every year at grandma's home for Diwali celebrations. They could be traditions having to do with family structure, such as having the family live together even as it grows, so that sons and their wives typically start their lives in the family home. Another tradition might be that when a woman gives birth, she spends a few weeks (usually forty days) at her parents' house, so that she can rest and receive an adequate amount of help.

A family's loyalties can be negative as well, and this can sometimes be traced as a generational practice that does not serve a family well. Examples might be that when big fights occur, people will cut off offending family members and may go for years without talking to each other. Another unhelpful family loyalty might be that men in the family make all of the decisions, or that girls in the family are not allowed to choose their own mates, while boys may have the privilege of doing so.

Genogram

When clients work with me, an important tool I use to explore their backgrounds is called a *genogram*, or diagram of a family tree. For those of you working on uncovering your own history, this is a great exercise to do. It helps us see *intergenerational transference*, the process of transferring mental or emotional thoughts, feelings, pain, patterns of behavior, and/or problems from one generation to the other. As part of this process, think about all of the tiny things that may have impacted you as you grew up. For a lot of people, these are memories of growing up in grandma's home, or in a different country. For example, many people remember a specific dining table, and the fun of eating together; others think of the foods that were considered treats, and the things that made life fun for them.

One person may say, "I remember growing up near my grandma's house in Pakistan. Both grandparents lived close enough that we could walk over from one place to the other. When the family got together, we had *tahiri* (or *tehri*, a spicy yellow rice cooked with potatoes and a tinge of saffron). It was my favorite. I could smell it from afar as soon as I took off my shoes and entered the house. To date, when I visit a family or friend's house and they have cooked it, I feel like I'm home."

The questions you want to think about in the genogram exercise are questions centering around how love was expressed, and what made it feel safe for you to love others. For a lot of people in the Indian sub-continent, food is the prime way to express love. When I talk to teenagers in my sessions, they often comment that their grandparents seldom give them tight hugs or that when they say, "I love you," it almost sounds fake. I explain to them that their grandparents' generation did not grow up with verbal affirmations, or physical expressions of love. A teenage girl told me that her grandfather blushed very strongly after she gave him a tight hug at the airport when he arrived from Delhi. He just smiled awkwardly at her, and she didn't understand why. Her mom explained that there were at least thirty other Indians around, and he felt self-conscious in front of them. Physical expression of love is not a common occurrence in that generation. Love was shown in action, expressed by cooked food, clean clothes, and family duties (such as taking care of the home's finances).

Attachment and Relationship with Parents and Caregivers

As you continue to explore the growing up part of your, I would like to introduce you to an important theory about how people function in their romantic relationships. This is called *attachment theory*. John Bowlby, a noted British psychologist and therapist who worked on child development and attachment issues, said that the close emotional bond formed between children and their caregivers is responsible for laying the foundation for the future bond that develops between adults later on. It does not matter whether the caregivers were biological parents, aunties, babysitters, or any other person. That first bonding is of vital importance for both emotional and romantic relationships in later life.

So, at this point it is important to understand who made you feel loved and safe in your childhood. As many say, who was your "person on the bench?" This person is the grown-up who encouraged you, loved on you, reassured you, and made you feel better. Sometimes it's more than one person, and sometimes you may not be able to identify any one individual. I will caution you that as South Asians, we tend to "glorify" our relationships a bit more than other cultures do. What this means is that we are a somewhat formal culture, and so we tend to report only good things about our family, society, country, and so on. This may sometimes get in our way of seeing things as clearly as we might. I often do initial sessions with clients who immediately say that their mom or dad made them feel loved, but then when I ask questions about how the love and reassurance was expressed, limited examples are given. Nevertheless, do identify your *attachment figures* (your "persons on the bench"), and we will touch on them later in this book.

If you had positive attachment relationships strongly present in your life, then you are highly likely to feel loved, secure, and confident in your adult relationships later on. Dr. Susan Johnson, a Canadian clinical psychologist and expert on couples' relationships, explains that those individuals who were securely attached to a caregiver when they were children tend to lean toward healthier relationships, In contrast, those who did not have this type of secure attachment may wind up questioning their relationships in adulthood, since trust may not come naturally to them. For example, if you are a girl who had a fantastic relationship with your father, then you have a higher chance of loving your husband with ease, giving him the benefit of the doubt and being forgiving when the need arises. The opposite may also be true. If you are a man who had a distressing relationship with your mother while growing up, then trusting your wife's intent may not come naturally to you in your marital relationship later on.

Another kind of attachment, called the *anxious-avoidant* type, stems from when inconsistent and unreliable care and attention are received from caregivers. This results in the child wanting to punish the caregiver while still craving to make an emotional connection with them. Once they are in an adult relationship, a person with this type of attachment may express a "come, come, – go away" cycle of wanting love and attention. Their spouses typically complain that when they give their mate attention, they get pushed away, but yet at other times their mate complains that they don't get <u>enough</u> attention!

Think about your attachment style and how it may have impacted your relationships in general. We will talk about this topic more in later chapters, as well.

Your Teenage Years

Your pre-teen and teenage years are an important part of your history, and it is critical to understand them. While we are experiencing puberty, most of our emotions tend to feel much more intense than they do at other times in our life. This intensity of feeling can remain with us and can even color the way we view people and relationships for the rest of our lives!

It is so natural to feel that type of intensity when we are teens. The first seeds of romance are sometimes rooted in these years. Whether you experience your first emotional crush, or your first sexual experience, these years are crucial to the development of many of the elements of who you are as a person.

Another aspect to notice when you think about your teen years are the sources of your conflicts and confusion. Who were the people with whom you argued? What made you angry? Who got under your skin? Who were the relatives you wanted to avoid, and who were the ones you always wanted to be around?

The human brain continues to grow and develop until the age of about 25 years old. It is our first experiences, though, that sometimes make the deepest impact upon us. As a result, in our teen years it is easy to get fixated on the one or two things that give us joy, and also on the one or two people with whom we feel conflicted. For example, this is the time you start steering toward having one friend who you always want to hang out with, or a special group of friends who you want to do things with all the time.

"Growing up, my immediate family was lower-middle class, but some of the extended family were upper-middle and upper class. So, while we got together at dinners and family outings and 'get-togethers,' I could not see the difference until we became teenagers. Then I wanted to buy stuff and do stuff. All the fun outings were with the cousins who were richer than us and I didn't have money and I didn't grow up with a voice where I could ask for things. I just knew I had responsibilities that I had to take care of when I grew up, and

if I asked for something all I could feel was guilt. I feel I created this identity for myself in those years. As a grown fifty-five-year-old man, I feel sad most of the time, and resentful sometimes. That's all I know."

Sibling Position

Dr. Walter Toman and Dr. Murray Bowen researched family systems and how birth order impacts personality development – in other words, the importance of where we fit among our brothers and sisters. Their conclusions are not set in stone, but nevertheless there are some generalizations that can be made. For example, first-born children have been found to have a tendency towards leadership and dominance, whereas younger siblings have a tendency towards *followership* (that is, the tendency to take a non-leadership position). Middle children in general seem to have stronger communication skills; they must communicate with both older and younger siblings and therefore seem to develop a more natural sense of diplomacy that the other siblings may not have. Youngest children also seem to have less of a natural muscle for caregiving.

How does this play out in human culture? As an example, a wife who was the oldest sibling growing up may find it easier to care for her family than a wife who was a younger child, because caregiving seems very natural to her. Similarly, a boss who is an older child may work exceptionally well with an assistant who is the youngest child, because both are working in a relationship whose power dynamics are familiar to them. However, two colleagues who have the same birth order position may struggle in their relationship at work, because they both try to exert the same level of dominance. This type of dynamic may even be observed in some marriages. A partner who is an oldest sibling may be most complementary with someone who is a youngest sibling, because the elder's tendency toward leadership may work well with the younger's tendency toward followership. And sometimes, spouses may struggle if they are both the youngest siblings in their families, as both may expect to be the center of attention, and even compete for it at times.

Relationship History

As you continue this discovery of your life and family history, I also would like for you to think about the history of any romantic relationships you have experienced. Romantic relationships have a tremendous impact on how we see ourselves, and discovering which components of our personalities unfold in these relationships can provide us with great insights.

"I never thought I was the jealous sort until I started dating her. Everything was fine but then I felt like it made me angry when she gave extra attention to anyone – friends, family, and even some kids. I wanted that attention all to myself. I felt like

I did so much for her, so why should anyone other than me have access to her attention? I created fights and arguments for no reason. I feel so stupid thinking about it now. My parents didn't give me much attention growing up. They were really nice, don't get me wrong. They provided for me and I had a comfortable home and material items provided for me. There was hardly any emotional validation though; there were no compliments or recognition of things I did well. So, when I got them from her, I was so hungry for more of it that it was hard to share that with anyone. She said it made her claustrophobic, and I lost her."

Conflict and Resulting Confusion

Another element to think about in this journey of self-discovery is the level of conflict you experienced growing up, both in terms of internal and external conflicts. Perhaps you faced conflict over your stance on cultural or religious values, or over what you wanted to do as a choice of career. I bring this up in this context because children in South Asian cultures historically have not been given much freedom in these areas. The freedom to make personal choices is a more Western cultural value, and not commonly found in collective cultures. A very tender balance exists between families imparting preferred cultural values or religious practices, versus exerting rigid control over a child's reason and logical thought. This balance is shown in families where you hear the "because" responses, such as, "Because you don't question faith,' or

"Because I'm your mother," or "Because we know what is good for you"! This rigid approach feeds into a child's overall sense of self-doubt, and this doubt then can hinder, or even stunt, emotional development.

Whether it was as simple as not being allowed to learn how to play music, or as complicated as being molested or abused, documenting what you've experienced is vital to this journey. Write it down in your journal so that you can document these primary conflicts. They may have occurred a long time ago, but they have a lot to do with what, and how, you feel now.

Me as It Relates to Them (the "Self in the Family System")

'Me' is an important person to think about. Yes, I'm talking about you! You are the 'self' in the family system. Our family affects how we feel and act, but how each one of us internalizes that dynamic process is unique to who we are, and that makes each of us a unique 'self'. The term for this process of becoming our unique selves is called *differentiation*. Differentiation is the reason that siblings born to the same parents, and raised in the same household, will turn out to be quite different.

The less developed or differentiated our sense of self is over our lifetime, the more influence others can have on how we function. Bowen explains that the poorly differentiated self depends a lot on others' acceptance and approval. These individuals quickly adjust themselves to what they think others believe, in order to please them. Or, these people tend to force their family members to conform to their impression of what is acceptable to the overall group, because they cannot stand to be thought of as out of step with the majority – even when what the majority thinks or wants is not helpful or logically correct.

Does this sound familiar? The collective nature of South Asian culture means that we tend to be generally more conforming. Even if we personally disagree with a belief or practice, we may not outwardly show that, for fear of "going against the grain" of the larger group and being thought of as disrespectful. Worrying about what others think is actually a form of "group think", and can become perpetuated in conforming families, where it becomes the default approach to problem-solving. This approach can result in the following type of thinking: groupthink.

Groupthink is generally defined as a thinking or decision that otherwise smart and well-intentioned individuals take due to the urge to conform. The group does not share their personal views, doubts and beliefs in the interest of the group as they value harmony more than rational thinking. An example would be a family being against their daughter marrying outside the community because an element that does not have to do with the person's character and commitment to the relationship; is different (Shia vs. Sunni, Brahman vs. a different caste, Punjabi vs. Gujarati and so on). In this case, while the brothers or sisters may see that the person is responsible and capable; going against the family wishes may not serve them well, or may not be worth the strain.

A moment for reflection...

Overall, it is very important for you to recognize your path thus far as you start paying attention to your current self and why you are the way you are. Your attachments, the family members you were around as well as your parents and siblings make a significant impact on your development and personality. Let us keep exploring.

CHAPTER 7

Key Concepts For Healthier Relationships

'I have learned that I have a lot to learn.'
— **Maya Angelou**

It doesn't matter if you were born in South Asia or elsewhere around the world, this chapter will hopefully help you understand so many elements of your family, relationships, and most importantly yourself. When I work with clients in my practice, I always wish I had the time to do a workshop where I would explain these elements of self and relationships so they would better understand these critical elements and how they play a part in relational dynamics. Reflect and think about your own self and your family history as you review them.

Cultures and Sub-Culture

Many experts have said that culture is defined as the set of values and beliefs societies have about how the world works. As a result of those values and beliefs, we figure out how to behave in society, at work, in our community, or at home in our relationships. Even within the South Asian community, culture can be a combination of many elements, each depending on many factors. For example, if you belong to a faith community, there will be a part of your values and culture that come from there. If you belong to a minority or majority ethnic group, then part of your culture will come from there, as well.

One unique aspect of culture is that it defines the issues of what activities are moral and what figures in society are trustworthy for that culture's members. The culture of a society defines a general sense of what is morally acceptable in a given situation, such as when dating in North America. While the overall culture may say that dating is a fine activity, dating maybe considered morally wrong within your family, as this is not a value to which your sub-culture subscribes. Similarly, the general consensus in North America is that if a situation appears suspicious or dangerous, the police should be called to provide protection. Many South Asians, however, come from cultures which hold the stereotype that police officers are corrupt and not trustworthy. People may feel that if they call the police the situation will escalate quickly into an unmanageable and out-of-control situation. Depending upon how long a family has lived in North America, their perspective on how to interact with law enforcement may vary widely. The concept of having simultaneous membership in multiple and conflicting cultures is an important one when it comes to understanding ourselves and our relationships. Now we can see how it is possible to have inside us two totally conflicting views of the same situation.

Bi-Cultural Identity and Adjusting

When we live in one country and have roots in another, we have a *bi-cultural identity*. Research shows that the dominant culture, regardless of whether it is the culture you live in or the culture you were born in, will influence your views on such things as sensitivity to important issues, goals you set, your definition of success, communication styles, and even your sense of humor. Eventually emigrant families will evolve over time to have integrated values that come from both cultures, in effect forming a third, separate culture within their own family unit

> *"I feel sad when I look at my family sometimes. When I came to America, I wanted a better life for myself, for my family back home, and for my future family. I worked so hard so I could be financially stable, have enough to support my parents, and to live a good life with my wife and children here. When they were younger, it was so much easier. They listened and accepted whatever values we gave them. Education is a big part of what me and my wife wanted to give our kids. We strongly believed that it would not only set them up for success but would also set them apart and give them the ability to help others and make a difference in this world. They would make us proud, just like we made our*

parents proud. Don't get me wrong, my kids are doing well. Some would say they are thriving. Then why is it that I feel a sense that something was lost on the way, when I see my daughter wearing shorts around the house, in front of my father sometimes? I feel this way when my son says he's busy and does not spend time with us, and when they refuse to join us for dinners and others' kids come. It almost seems like my kids want to spend less and less time with us. The family nights and dinners are few and far between. I feel like I have lost that connection with them that I had when they were younger. I wonder if we lost our values in attempting to get our children well-educated?"

Collective Cultural Roots versus Individualistic Orientation

Time and again, I hear from teenagers and young adults that they wonder who these "people" or "loag" are that are so important for their parents' to have approval about. They also question why they can't just live life the way they want to. This sense of being too tightly controlled is largely rooted in the individualistic orientation of North America coming into conflict with the collective roots of South Asian culture. Collective values, such as sacrificing your personal wishes for the good of the family, are not only admired in desi culture, but are also considered to be a realistic expectation of children and adults who come from so-called "good families."

Loosely explained, individualism promotes personal freedom of choice and rewards individual achievement.

Collectivism considers achievement to be really an achievement for the family, and it gives credit to them over the individual. There is more emphasis on conformity than on one person standing out above others. Examples of collectivism include the pressure a son may feel if he wants to move out of the family home and live with his wife and his own family. Or if a girl does not want to wear conservative clothing when the rest of the girls are more conservatively dressed, then she will stand out and cause anxiety for the family. If a boy wants to be an artist rather than pursue a technical career, it may be frowned upon, especially if everyone else in the family works in a technical field.

Privileges – Looks, Family, Money, Class, Education, Gender, Citizenship

The level of privilege in a South Asian family makes a huge difference as to how strongly that family is affected by traditional beliefs and values. This privilege could consist of many things: education, financial standing, social status, or immigration status, to name a few. Look at it this way: You may have noticed that more educated families tend to have a more liberal approach towards how their girls behave, especially as to how much liberty they are allowed. The girls may be allowed to go out more, or to stay out later, or even to socialize in a mixed group. This obvious difference between families creates serious discord among young people, as they may notice girls from some families in their community socializing much more than others are allowed to do. This kind of selective family morality can drive desi kids crazy in their growing-up years!

Increased socio-economic status affords many privileges to families, but it also carries with it a noticeable social pressure for a family's children to behave perfectly in all situations. This pressure is made worse by the fact that wealthier families have so much visibility in the South Asian community. In desi communities, a wealthy family is not necessarily also a liberal one. They may still carry on many conservative practices from back home, and have higher expectations from their children, because they <u>very</u> much do not want it to look like they are taking the privilege of their wealth for granted. The stress generated by these privileges can create severe social conflicts both within and between families, and may exceed the ability of families to deal with them.

Psychological/Emotional Concepts about Self and Relationships

So far we have seen how the conflicts you experience may have had a social influence because of our culture, its collective thinking, selective family morality, and values/beliefs about trust. However, there are some additional key elements of the dynamics within your South Asian family that may intensify the conflicts you have experienced. Below, I will introduce you to the concepts of *codependence* and *boundaries*. As a matter of fact, these concepts are so important that they may come into play in any family, regardless of their country of origin.

Codependence in the Cultural Context

If you decide to google the term *codependence* most of the explanation you see will be anchored in concepts related to addictive behaviors, especially in relation to families where one person has an addiction (of any type) and their family member or romantic partner does not. However, I want to apply the term *codependence* to a type of behavior that I have seen consistently in South Asian families – and I have worked with hundreds of them! This will help us understand some of the dysfunctional relationships we see in the South Asian family systems.

So, what is our definition of codependence? Codependence occurs when a person has too much emotional and/or psychological dependence on a partner or family member. This partner is needed to meet all of the first person's needs for emotional support and self-esteem. This reliance is excessive, to the extent that nearly all of a person's emotional needs must be met by this one other person. (Poor *boundaries*, which I will talk about next, are a classic symptom of codependent relationships.) The needy person consistently seeks rescue from the other family member, and the dysfunction just goes on and on within the family system. Let me help you see this with a classic example.

If a child in the family seems to get what they want whenever they throw a tantrum, it gives that child the message that this kind of behavior is what he needs to do in order to get what he wants. If he is a stubborn child, he will keep repeating his behavior despite being corrected, and so just to shut him up, the parents may give in to get some relief. All this drama occurs while other siblings watch their brother getting away with behaviors they could never get away with, and this builds a lot of resentment against the parents. The other siblings feel they are being treated unfairly. Chaos grows, and the needy child starts feeling both convinced that he must throw a tantrum in order to get what he wants, as well as entitled to special attention. When he becomes an adult and gets into a romantic relationship, he will expect the same special attention from his spouse. He needs his spouse to solve his problems and focus on his needs, while he continually dismisses her needs. He must remain loyal to his victimhood! He needs another person to meet his needs, whether it be a parent or a wife. This will eventually fatigue the spouse, and the only way she might know to get relief from the chaos is to have an affair or leave the relationship.

In the above example, the needy person is codependent, but the parents and spouse are enablers and are also considered codependent. The enablers get a sense of identity and purpose from rescuing the dysfunctional person who is not able to regulate his needs on his own. It takes "two to tango" in this dance because the codependent partners do not have a good sense of self – in other words, they have poor *boundaries*.

Boundaries

Simply explained, *boundaries* are the limits in emotional, physical, or mental "space" where your unique sense of self ends and where another's sense of self begins. You have boundaries between yourself and your parents, you and your friends, and also between you and your romantic partners. Does this sound confusing? It is like tuning in to your feelings and figuring out your comfort zone. For example, when you go out with your friends, your social boundary may be a willingness to go out for dinner, hookah, or a coffee. However, if they go out to a bar or a dance club, then that might feel uncomfortable for you - and so you realize that is where your personal boundary lies for activities with them. If you push yourself to go clubbing with them, you may have a greater chance of feeling uncomfortable than of actually enjoying yourself. And if you wind up not enjoying yourself, you even may develop resentment toward the friend who forced you to go! Boundaries are powerful limits that can have a big impact on our behaviors.

A *boundary* would separate your sense of self from that of others with whom you have relationships. For example, your boundary might feel imposed upon if you find your spouse demanding you participate in an activity that you are not comfortable doing. It may be relational, as when your spouse wants you to call his/her mother, claiming that is your duty. Or it may be a sexual boundary, if your partner wants to engage in sexual acts that feel out of your comfort zone.

It is important to understand that going to a social event, reaching out to family, or sexual exploration within a relationship are all acceptable stretches of a person's comfort zone. The difference between exploring out of your comfort zone and a boundary violation occurs when you are forced to do something for which you are not ready, or willing. The power imbalance that comes with not being ready is what feels wrong or bad. For example, perhaps your spouse attacks your character if you refuse to call your in-laws, or perhaps your partner insinuates that you must be a horrible wife because you will not participate in certain sexual acts.

Power is a critical component of both healthy and unhealthy relationship dynamics in a family. Sometimes this dynamic is obvious, because one member is the bottleneck, or powerhouse, where all power resides in the family. In these cases that person is usually male, although sometimes it also may be a female. If this powerhouse agrees with whatever is being proposed, then everything is fine - but if he/she is not okay with it, then you could turn blue trying to convince him/her, but it simply will not happen! For example, if the dad or mom has power or influence and they approve of a boy marrying outside the culture, it is acceptable.

A moment for reflection...

As you read this chapter, I invite you to think about your families, your relationships, your friendships as well as your work life. Many of these elements may present themselves in different settings of your life. Keep discovering.

CHAPTER 8

Confessions And Secrets: Being Brave To Reveal And Re-Evaluate

'..Turn your wounds into wisdom.'

— Oprah Winfrey

This chapter is about secrets and pain. Secrets are heavy and may give you anxiety. When you think about telling someone, it may make you feel sick to your stomach. These are elements of your life that you have not shared with anyone, or perhaps have only shared with one or two others. Sometimes you just carry on with your life, minimizing the secret and trying not to focus on it. You concentrate on feeling grateful for what you have. At other times, you feel that if you face the issue, you will fall apart - so you don't want to go into that space. There are so many people near and dear to you who would be impacted if they knew about this secret, so you refuse to do anything about it. Here are some examples of secrets and they pain they can cause in our lives. See if they resonate with your particular situation. I'll talk to you again at the end of the chapter to check in.

I hate my parents.

"It is very frustrating not to be able to explain to my parents why I don't want to be around them. They don't understand that we are not living in India. We live in America. Every time I sit with them, it becomes a lecture series – a sermon. They don't know how to be. It's either a fear of something I will do because they heard about it from their friends (who need a life!), or it's a fear that I should be doing something that I am not. I feel like they transfer their anxiety to me, and I suddenly feel inadequate. By the way, if I haven't said so, I hate being compared to other people's kids and what they have accomplished. Geez, it's too much. When I see my parents, I want to run in the opposite direction. The less time we spend together, the better it is."

Sex- what is that?

"We have not had sex in four years. My husband says he doesn't feel like it. We have not been naked, and our bodies have not touched in longer than that. I crave touch. Living in America, when I hear all the stories of how many positions my friends have tried, and what their spouses like to do, and how they cannot get enough - I just feel inadequate! I start wondering if he is attracted to me. I wonder if he is having an affair. I wonder if I should have an affair. I can't tolerate it when he compliments other women. He barely notices me. It hurts so much. I wonder if not having a sex life would qualify as a reason for divorce. When I asked him if he feels desire, he

said no. He said he is usually so tired, so he doesn't feel desire. I know he is lying because I've felt the bed shake when he is relieving himself. I pretend to be asleep, but so many times I've wanted to turn and join him. I feel so hopeless."

I'm considered a sin... being desi and gay...

When I came to the U.S., I realized there are others like me. It would make me so uncomfortable when my family would want me to look at possible girls to be arranged for marriage. Doing well here, there was more and more pressure. I told my sister, thinking she would understand. We were always close, but she got so angry and told me that I have lost my values and she thinks I am disgusting. She said she will struggle to get a good proposal if I come out publicly, and that if I love her, I have to keep my identity concealed. I am in a healthy relationship with my partner, but I can never imagine taking him home or meeting my family. It's like I had to give up my culture, my family, my roots, and my celebrations, just because of how my family would be shamed in society. A part of me has died."

Proud to be ABCD

"I am an American first; yes, with desi roots. Sometimes I feel that living in the pro-women's liberation world is a façade because it does not apply to me. I cannot play sports because I'm a girl. I cannot hang out in groups if boys are there, too. My brother can go out with friends, but I cannot. If I talk to a boy, I must be dating him! I am not free to do anything without having some kind of limitation. I feel claustrophobic. It's like my future career is a hobby till I find a husband and then he will decide whether I can have a career or not. Then they wonder why I hate my culture."

Feeling like a failure on both ends... is it social pressure or ADD?...

"I was worried about her but now I'm tired of it. There are some days she doesn't get out of bed. I tell her to have a schedule and be productive. She does nothing around the house. When I sit her down to explain to her that she should get her act together, she seems to agree when I talk to her. She seems to get it, but then that is it – nothing happens. I'm the one taking care of the kids when I get home and I clean up. Sometimes the house looks like a hurricane hit it. She's so obsessed with Facebook and spends most of her time stalking other people. Then I hear about how this friend went on this vacation and this friend's husband bought her a Louis Vuitton and has a full-time nanny. The demands are never-ending. I work hard and long hours. To come home and hear the complaints about what we don't have is just intolerable. She compares me to all these amazing husbands and then expects me to have sex with her. It's not going to happen. Sometimes I feel she doesn't even notice me. I am a paycheck and feel stuck. I'm getting ready to say I'm done."

Dr. Sheeza Mohsin

Looking for the perfect girl..

"She lived in the flats (apartments) right across from us in Bangalore, and I would often see her on the balcony when she helped her mom hang clothes on the clothesline to dry. She was so perfect, wearing simple clothes and nothing fancy. Life was so simple. One time, she looked at me and burst out laughing. I was so embarrassed. My friend told me that she later told her friend my mouth was open so big when I stared at her that she could see my tonsils. I knew she was smart. I am thirty-three years old and I feel like I'm chasing that innocence when I flip through pictures of girls on dating apps here. I'm so successful and a fairly good catch, but I seek her essence in my partner. How stupid is that?"

My child is special needs... this pain that will never go away...

"On most days, I'm fine. We have a good life and the health insurance benefits with my husband's job are great. We can get all the services we need for our daughter. I can't believe she's fourteen now and doing so much better than she was just a few years ago - but a piece of me died when she got diagnosed with autism. I didn't have a sister and I had so many dreams about how my daughter would be my friend when she grows up. That is what I thought when she was born. For the past ten years or so I feel this is all we do. We plan doctor visits, and appointments for some kind of therapy, and some treatment plan that needs attention. My marriage

suffers sometimes. I have no energy for sex. I feel so terrible for my son because he has to do everything with his sister in mind. Our social life was so impacted when the kids were growing up. We would not be invited to parties because people did not want to put up with her acting out. I feel so angry sometimes, especially at family members who knew but weren't there for us. It hurts so much. I feel so inadequate and sad."

Never enough...

"He does love me I think. He just gets mad when I don't listen to him. As long as I do everything, he seems okay most of the time. Sometimes though, I just feel like I could do everything he wants me to, but it is still not enough. He doesn't like socializing. He criticizes pretty much everyone we meet. If someone is more successful than us, he definitely doesn't like them. It hurts when he picks on me in front of the kids. He says my family did not raise me well enough to do many things that I'm trying hard to learn. He fought with me so hard when I disagreed with him. I feel very anxious around him. It's like I don't know who I'm going to interact with – the good person or the mean person. I work hard and try to manage all I can, but it seems to be never enough"

My parents are my life...

"Why is it that we are only responsible for taking care of his parents, when mine are in need of support as well? I feel a lot

of resentment because I have been taking care of them for so long. No one else steps up – none of his brothers or sisters. My mother wants to come spend time with me, but I have no privacy. I've never experienced my own nuclear family without my in-laws. I feel so much anger when people praise my husband for taking care of his parents when I'm the one who takes care of them. Don't get me wrong, they are nice people, but sometimes I just crave being by myself. I don't want to have someone witness what I do and don't do in the house all the time. I'm tired."

I'll forgive you... one more time...

"I feel so ashamed of myself. I have no spine. I feel pathetic. I have caught him so many times – messages, bills, and trips. He promises me he will leave her, but it doesn't happen. She creeps in our lives again like a fungus that just keeps growing on your toe. Every time I threaten to leave, he begs me to stay and points me in the direction of the kids and how much he cares for me. He's a good provider and a good father. He works so hard and I see that, but this jabs in my heart each time I think about them on a trip or exchanging love notes. Then he tells me I'm his best friend. Best friend? It's been twenty years and I'm still struggling with this. What a life I've wasted. I should have left when I found out, but the kids were so little. He says he's left her, but I don't trust him. Suspicion is eating me inside. I get into these obsessive phases when I yell at him and he listens. I feel terrible after that, but I can't

help it. He keeps telling me it's over but what is the point? Fifteen years ago, I was young, and I had options. What do I do with myself now but live with that resentment?"

Sleeping with the enemy

"He's a successful entrepreneur and so dynamic. He does so many great things for our community. He is well-respected and is considered such a prominent figure. But he can be a monster to me. I get to be the special one – the special one who sees his dark side. Once he starts drinking and can't stop, the monster comes out. The time he pulled me by my hair and dragged me across the slippery marble floor to our room, I could feel my hair separating from my scalp! My mother-in-law heard, I know, because the door to her bedroom shut right when I was being dragged in front of it. I saw the shadow of her feet. She didn't come out. On lucky nights, it would end at the beatings. On those bad, torturous nights, it would end with a rape. I would live in a zone for a few days after. He would be so kind those days. He would bring me flowers and love on me and kiss me in the kitchen when I was cooking, like we were the happily married couple from the movies. I want out. I am scared he will kill me. He has threatened to do that. I'm really scared."

Yes, I am gay...

"I am gay – maybe even stereotypically gay. I have known since I was nine years old because of so many reasons. I was *bullied in school and considered different. I felt safer interacting with girls because I enjoyed the non-sporty things they did. I love fashion and was always into designing clothes and noticing how people dressed up. My first crush was on a boy in my class when I was twelve. He became my best friend and he was all I wanted to be around. We had a strong platonic friendship. I was devastated when he fell in love with a girl in his neighborhood. I felt betrayed and did not even know how to react. "*

Divorce is not the solution...

"How can she divorce him? What will others think? What will become of her younger sisters of marriageable age? People will think they must be uncompromising like her, and no one will want to marry them. In our family, girls don't abandon their marriages. It is a side effect of too much education and being able to earn. I was telling her father to not let her study so much. This is the last thing I need to see before I die!"

He's not one of our own...

"I love him, and he loves me. He's not from my faith but he understands me more than anyone has ever understood me. He's so different from my father and brothers. He didn't even want to kiss me when we first met alone, because he said he knew I'm from a conservative family and he didn't want to disrespect me. My brothers disrespect me every day. We live in America, but they think I am a girl so I should pick up at

the table and wash dishes and iron their clothes because they are the men of the house. They don't show any compassion.

They only know how to show control and to protect the family honor by controlling me. This is not the teaching of our faith. When mom found out, she said my brothers will kill me, and then kill him. Part of me believes that. I'm scared for us. I know we will have such a beautiful life together. He said I don't even have to change my religion. He accepts me for who I am. He said I should consider going to college because he wants an educated wife who will raise our children. I feel valued by him. My aunt and her lover were killed in honor killings back home. My brothers made a statement some time ago that she deserved it."

Drugs… He uses, and says it's not a big deal

"I don't know what to do. When I first caught him, he was smoking weed in his room. He keeps telling me I'm so boring and old fashioned and that everybody does it. We have a daughter and sometimes when he gets high, he acts out and tries to engage in fights, and then blames me, in her presence. It becomes my fault. I have thought of leaving the relationship so many times but my family will be heart broken. I don't want my child to grow up without a father. I love him but I'm so angry at him. This is not what I signed up for! I feel helpless."

Shh... it's going to be our secret...

"I was 10 years old when he starting touching me. He would find every opportunity when I was alone and tell me it's our secret. In the bathroom and at home. He knew when my mom was out and when my dad was not there. He was my grandfather. I was supposed to be safe with him. What hurt the most was my mom telling me not to tell anyone. I get angry every time I see him. I resent her. When I told my cousin, she told me her mother was sexually abused by her own brother. How can they sleep at night? I want to get him arrested. I don't care."

Being married to two people.. The trauma of Mental Illness..

"No, he doesn't beat me. To the best of my knowledge he's not having an affair. My reality lies in being married to two people. When the nice one shows up, we are a loving family bursting with jokes and laughter and hugs. He has perspective and is forgiving. I start thinking this is the reason I married him. This is the man I love. This is the man I will stand by, through thick and thin."

How are you feeling?

Are you wondering if this is real or are you relating to one of these issues as similar to your own? Are you realizing the deep pain that people carry and still wake up every day and face the world with courage and grace and wondering how they do it? Are you wondering if there is any recovery from pain such as the examples above?

I want to invite you to feel hope that there is. I have had the honor of working with countless brave souls and the pleasure of helping them work through their trauma, pain or relationship challenges so they can have clarity, peace and contentment. You just have to be committed to putting an effort in healing and repairing. Then the magic happens. You will need knowledge, skills and a focus on wanting better. Let me show you some ways to do that. Read on…

'Our greatest joy and our greatest pain comes from our relationships with others'.

Stephen Covey

DISCLAIMER: Please note that the situations and people described in this chapter are composites of my professional experience, to protect the privacy of those who have shared with me. For those of you who have shared with me, please know that the example didn't make it in the book if it was just a single report. Many others would have to share the challenge, which is how I prioritized which examples to share.

Also, the information I share about South Asians does not represent "hard and fast" dictates about the entire population. This is my perspective based on my learning, training and experience.

STAGE TWO

Preparing To Change

CHAPTER 9

Introduction To Stage Two – Preparing To Change

"It is not the strongest of the species that survives, nor the most intelligent, but the one most responsive to change."

— **Charles Darwin**

"I am a little bit in shock and a little overwhelmed, to be honest. I can't believe that I was oblivious to so many elements of the life that I experienced. It's like going to Paris and traveling inside a bus that you never leave. You just experience life from afar and don't pause at stops to take stock and change course if need be. You don't stop for a restroom visit to relieve yourself, or for lunch so you can nurture yourself. You experience all this from a distance. With so many fears of the unknown, it seemed better that way. At least that is what I thought.

Well, I'm in Paris again, and this time it's going to be different. I am making all the stops I want or need to. I will sit in experiences and absorb them. This trip is different. I'm already feeling stronger thinking about it. I feel like I will not be scared anymore."

What to Expect in This Stage

You have come this far through whatever you've had the strength and capacity to discover, and I am so elated to see you at this stage of your journey! Going through your personal and family history can be overwhelming. Some clients have told me they feel like they have these explosions in their brain, where they notice many minute elements of themselves that they never even knew existed. It is like sorting and cleaning out a closet after so many years. There is a lot of material to sort through, and a lot of decisions to make about what you find.

What Will Help You

One thing that so many of my clients have said helped them was having me tell them to slow down as they go through this process. Don't look at this journey as a project that you need to complete by the end of summer, or by the end of the year. Slowing down will help you be more deliberate, and to think carefully about what you need to do with these new emotions and feelings you have found. You don't need to make decisions about them right away!

If you don't slow down, your first impulse for what to do with these emotions will become your go-to response. If you are the type of person who avoids unpleasant feelings, then you will start ignoring and minimizing your new emotions. If you have an assertive personality style, you may feel the urge to immediately confront the people who may have wronged you, or perhaps to have a painful conversation with a parent that they are not ready to have. Or you could simply freeze and feel like you are numb, compartmentalizing and moving on like you always do. It is important to avoid all of these behaviors because they are defense mechanisms your mind uses to relieve your discomfort with your new feelings. Instead, you need to "sit with" your feelings for a while, and stay mindful of them. Delaying taking action can help give you the time you need to make wiser decisions.

What Rewards May Come Your Way

Life gets in the way of this emotional work. Many benefits exist to being an adult. For the most part, we can do what we want – but many of us have been conditioned to believe that we do not really have that liberty. Many times, when clients are in this stage of their journey, they tell me that our session feels like a great luxury. They have the chance to think only about themselves, without feeling guilty or obliged to do something else. They feel our sessions are an indulgence because most of us raised in a South Asian household are conditioned to think of others' needs before our own. We think of others, accommodate others, take care of others' feelings, and make sure that others are cared for first. To us, being kind to ourselves is not an option that we think we have.

How to Be Kind to Yourself in This Stage of Work

One of the biggest gifts you can give yourself is the gift of time. I know your response is that you barely have time for anything. In fact, sometimes you're not even sure where your day went! You are a servant to the schedule of whatever needs to be done, and you wish there were just a few extra minutes somewhere in the day so you could do what you <u>want</u> to do for a change – instead of what you <u>have</u> to do or what you feel you are required to do. Although this might not make sense initially, I suggest combatting these feelings with some of the self-care activities below. Please trust me; these activities will become crucial to the sustained progress of your journey over time.

Recommendations for Self-Care

I invite you to start journaling regarding how you spend your time. This is called keeping a "time log." A time log is actually a type of mindfulness exercise, and it provides amazing results. It is similar to having a food journal, or a spreadsheet for how you spend your money. Until you start noticing how you use time as a resource you will not know whether your time is truly being used or just wasted.

Let me give you an example. In family financial counseling, my professor explained that what often gets in the way of a family feeling relaxed and secure is constantly "living beyond their means". I thought I couldn't be one of those people, because I didn't buy designer clothes or take frequent vacations. I thought I was working to increase my income so I could get to the point where I could save money eventually. My professor offended me at first, because he told me I was wrong; he said that if you can't save money on your present income, then you won't be able to save with a higher income, either! Saving or managing money is a muscle that has to be exercised. If you don't use it, you'll get in the habit of overspending and find yourself trapped in a cycle of poverty. People who are financially comfortable are that way more because of how they spend save their money, than because of how much money they make. And the same is true with time!

Start noticing how you spend your time, and write it down on your phone or in your calendar. For example, when you spend time on social media, just put it on your e-calendar like an appointment! Use a specific color for time-wasters like social media, and random calls that you take, or for T.V., Netflix time, etc. Use a different color to code when you do important things, like take walks, work out, prepare healthy meals, or spend focused and un-interrupted time with your children.

In doing this, you are looking for how your time gets sucked down the drain via trivial activities. These "time sucks" keep you from doing other things that truly give you joy and contentment. And it is the activities that give you joy and contentment that also provide you with self-care! (Naps, hot showers, and cuddle time with my kids are high on my personal self-care list.) Start thinking now about what those activities might be for you, and how much you will enjoy being able to do them once your "time sucks" have been identified and conquered. So, the next time you pick up a random phone call with someone (who called at what was a good time for them, not you), remember that this was an example of a "time suck" – and resolve to avoid such a situation the next time it happens.

And finally, one of the most important things you can do is to continue this journey of self-discovery in the company of an objective therapist, either myself or someone else. There are countless benefits to utilizing a therapist, counselor, or coach to support you through this journey. Change requires hard work. Having a guide, confidant, and most importantly, a skilled professional who understands the tough journey of making and sustaining change, can be invaluable for your journey towards a better self.

Remember, change happens over time. Life doesn't stop because you are working on yourself. You have to continue to do what you need to in life, but you can commit to doing it more mindfully, so you notice how you're spending your valuable time. Good luck!

CHAPTER 10

Discovering Why You're Stuck

'Change is never painful; it is the resistance to change that is painful.'

— Buddha

In this chapter I ask you to start thinking about why you may be stuck in your current problematic situation. After reading the previous chapter, you may have written down the issues that are struggles for you, and may have already noticed a pattern in your challenges. Every time you have attempted change, something kept you stuck in the dysfunction or the situation. Here are some possible explanations, based in a familiar South Asian context, for why this might be. Remember that your situation may be one or more of these; some of our challenges are more complex than others!

Learned Helplessness

Martin Seligman is an American psychologist who performed research on a behavior he called *learned helplessness*. This behavior explains the saga of conflict within many South Asian families. Here is how it works. The common power dynamic in most South Asian families is to have one or two key members (usually a parent or an older sibling) who have much more power than anyone else. In such a situation, when you are not the powerhouse member, your needs may consistently get denied. Eventually you may shut down emotionally, and no longer even try to get your needs met. You have learned to be helpless. Witnessing your experience may even encourage other family members to become helpless, too!

Why should I even try? I see what happened to my sister. No one ever gets out of this house.

Let's learn from the example of a common practice that is not culturally encouraged, even when we live in North America: marrying outside desi culture. If a parent showed extreme resistance in not allowing an older sibling to marry an outsider, and this created chaos in the family, then there is a good chance that other family members will not even attempt such an act. This is true even if the personalities involved seem like they might be a more acceptable match to the parents the second time the situation arises. This type of situation creates an ongoing tension in the family, and family members give up on trying to find opportunities for relief or change.

Another example of learned helplessness is when a person looking for a job is not doing much to train themselves, learn new skills, nor being flexible about the kind of job she/he will accept. They may find themselves internalizing that there is no hope, and that they must be being discriminated against because they are a minority. Please know that while discrimination clearly exists, and prejudiced behavior towards minorities occurs in many instances, it is not always the case. However, this notion can lead a person to avoid trying or acknowledging how their own behavior (such as not being adequately trained, not being competent in the English language, or other controllable factors) may get in their way of securing employment.

Karpman's Triangle

Another important concept we can use to understand dysfunction in your situation or struggle is that of Karpman's drama triangle. In the late 1960s, Stephen Karpman explained that relationships with unhealthy dynamics have three basic roles that family members play over and over again. These roles can rotate, keeping the problem going and even strengthening it over time. These roles are Victim, Rescuer, and Persecutor. These roles define the interaction (the *transaction*) between the family members as they play out what is basically "good guy versus bad guy", sometimes for decades.

The Victim in the family typically feels oppressed and helpless, powerless in changing their situation. They need help, and often seem like the person everyone in the family must support with solving their problems. Victims usually lack insight on how they may contribute to their own situation. The "poor me" and "you could never understand what I've gone through" positions are standards for this individual. An example would be someone in the family who has experienced major adversity. The Victim could be a family member in a bad marriage, or who is divorced, is chronically ill, or has lost a job. This role becomes their new job – powerlessness and helplessness.

The Rescuer is the family member who repeatedly enables the victim's negative behavior. They usually feel guilty if they don't rescue the victim, and they need a distraction from solving their own problems, so they keep the victim dependent and give him/her permission to fail. The Rescuer often gets validation from others for being helpful and big-hearted, and feels good about being needed. The Rescuer in the above example would be the parent, who may emotionally validate the adult child with the bad marriage, giving them more love and pity. This feels good for the victim, so he or she continues being the Victim. The Rescuer also could be multiple family members who are helping the divorced Victim financially, or with other resources, so that the Victim can continue avoiding employment and keep living beyond their means. Typically, the motivations of the Rescuer are the least obvious, and there is some hidden motive that pays off for her or him on a deeper psychological level. A parent Rescuer may feel validated and needed by the Victim, giving them purpose, and sometimes even strengthening their own victimhood.

The Persecutor role is usually identified as the "bad guy". She or he may be angry and express controlling and oppressive behavior. Persecutors frequently use blame in their language, and present as rigid and righteous. In the examples explained above, this would be the parent who refuses to give money to the child who is not making an effort to be independent, or the sibling who calls out the victimhood of their sibling. Persecutors seem to have more power in family relationships, and seem to take undue advantage of that power.

The intensity of the conflict in these triangles usually increases when the Persecutor is punished by the Victim, causing the Persecutor to turn into a Victim themselves. An example would be if a parent refused to let their daughter marry someone of her choosing, and then the daughter eloped, making her parents the victims of societal shame. The new spouse is now a Rescuer in this system, and can also become the Victim, blaming the parental Persecutor for being so harsh as to drive the daughter to take such a drastic step in the first place.

Irrational Thoughts

In the psychological world the *if/then* and *abundance/scarcity mentalities* are called *cognitive distortions*. *Cognitive distortions* are inaccurate, irrational, negative thoughts that people tend to repeat to themselves. Since the goal of this book is to get you started on your own therapeutic journey, I am attempting to teach you these terms so that you can search them later, in case you want to move to a deeper level of understanding about them. Irrational thoughts come from the same part of our brain as the rational thoughts which allow us to think critically, so it can be hard to believe that we can think irrational things, but most of us do have some cognitive distortions. We'll talk about them in the section that follows.

When repetitive thinking patterns hurt us, or our relationships, it is time to question them and try to understand why we think that way. Sometimes faulty connections are made in our brain when we link together two things that happened around the same time. These things may be related, or they may not be. Either way, our brains have made the connection, and we need to figure out if it is a real connection or an irrational thought. Below are some examples of this kind of irrational thinking (cognitive distortion), using the setting of our South Asian culture. I've drawn my explanations for these from the pioneering work of psychiatrists Dr. Aaron Beck and Dr. David Burns.

One type of cognitive distortion is "black and white thinking". For South Asian parents, an example would be the belief that hanging out with American children is damaging for our kids. The truth of the matter is that not all children are bad <u>or</u> good, regardless of whether they are inside or outside of our community. The inability to see grey, or any shades of variation, is an example of distorted thinking. When someone in the community struggles with an adverse experience, such as a child or teen struggling with drugs or suicide, our cultural group-think may overgeneralize and say that theirs is not a "good family." This belief is a distortion of the truth, and causes unnecessary pain for the family currently suffering with the pain of this problem. What is objectively true is that not all members of a family have the same outlook, personality, or problems, and it is a distortion of reality to make all family members out to be the same. Similarly, another type of distortion views everything in a situation through either a positive or a negative "mental filter", focusing on just one attribute about a person, family, or situation. Using such a filter, we might believe that just because someone's dad is a doctor, the family must be "nice" people, or that they come from a "good family." This is the same dangerous filter that feeds negative stereotypes about entire communities, such as, "Muslims are terrorists."

"Fortune-telling" or jumping to conclusions is another cognitive distortion. With this type of thinking, a person may feel that they can forecast or predict what is going to happen in a particular situation. If you've been in many romantic relationships, you may feel strongly that you know what you like or dislike in a partner, and you may quickly decide yes or no on a potential partner based on only limited knowledge about them. You may "fortune tell" in this way: *"I know I'll never find love again. I've seen this happen over and over again. It's hopeless... I'm hopeless!"*

"Fortune-telling" can quickly become catastrophizing or minimizing, and this is a trait that desi families seem to have a knack for, in my experience. If a child gets a bad grade or does not get into the college of their choice, the family may view this event as a disaster and label it as a catastrophe. Minimizing happens when spouses or parents cannot relate to something that is intensely felt by another family member, such as the loss of a job, like the dissolution of a friendship. It is a devastating event for you, and yet your family members will quickly tell you to move on; they may even get impatient if you talk about it "too much." What you then might hear in these cases are "should" statements that can be quite emotionally damaging to the recipient, causing both anger and resentment. You might hear, "You should be over it by now", or "You must call them and apologize because you disrespected them." This type of fortune-telling is also a form of codependent behavior, because unmet expectations lead to disappointment on one side, with resulting guilt or shame for not meeting those expectations on the other side. Again, it takes two partners to do this dance.

Another, quite dangerous distortion that most (if not all) of us have been affected by is that of translating intensely experienced feelings as inaccurate facts. We then judge a person or an event irrationally based on the filter that emotion creates. If you were not invited to a party by someone, or were not asked to take a picture with the bride and groom at a wedding you attended, then you may feel unimportant and insulted. You might minimize everything else that may have been positive about the experience, and view the entire event through a negative filter. These feelings can be harbored by families for years, and tend to show up often for South Asian families during weddings and funerals.

Or perhaps you heard your father yell at your sister about going out with friends, and so you assume that doing the same is definitely not an option for you to pursue with your parents; this makes you feel inferior to other kids. What you may not know is that conversation happened at the moment when your father received an upsetting phone call, and that completely influenced his attitude to your sister. You have made an irrational connection and internalized the feeling that you are not good enough. Cognitive distortion strikes again!

Balancing Heritage and Suffering – Internal Conflict

Like people, cultures can perpetuate very heavy messages and expectations that are rooted in cognitive distortions, generating serious emotional baggage for members of that group. Some examples are given below. Feel free to note the ones you have experienced in your own life, or observed within your family.

- My parents are living at home with me. I am a bad son because I really would rather not take care of them.

(Cultural expectation is that children will always want to take care of their elderly parents.)

- My parents don't live with me because it's hard for them and my nuclear family to get along with each other. I am a big disappointment to my parents (Cultural expectation is that multi-generational families should all live together and get along well.)
- I couldn't stay in my marriage because he was emotionally abusive to me. I should have been able to tough it out. Now I have brought shame to my family. (Cultural expectation is that wives will put up with whatever happens inside their marriage, no matter how abusive, because the husband is always right.)
- I am not as financially wealthy as the rest of my siblings. I am a failure. (Cultural expectation is that privilege is bestowed on all members of a family equally. If it is not, then it must be due to a personal failing.)

Understanding the Spectrum of Truth in your Bi-Cultural Identity

In general, a bi-cultural identity provides us with both a rich heritage and a major struggle. This struggle is ongoing, and we are faced daily with the fact that there is a spectrum of truth about almost everything in our lives. All our values and beliefs can be viewed through one or more competing lenses. The emotional stress from this competition can take a serious toll on our health and emotional well-being.

It's the struggle men have when they don't have their parents living with them due to the cultural expectation that the son will care for them. The struggle also shows up when they want their spouse to be both a modern female outside the house as well as a stereotypical South Asian wife in the home. It's the challenge women face when they have to put a child in daycare, and they feel like a bad mother every morning when they say good-bye. And as we have seen, this bi-cultural struggle occurs when teens try to assert their individuality while growing up, and are repeatedly shut down because "We don't do that in our family." How can you move forward from these conflicts?

Time to take stock

Write an impact letter to express all of the emotions you feel that have been hard for you to communicate in person. Addressing one letter to each of the family members with whom you have had major conflicts in your life is an activity I often do with my clients. If you struggled with a child doing drugs, a spouse struggling with mental illness, or a parent with a strained relationship, tell each one in a separate letter how the challenge of your relationship with them has impacted you and caused you grief. The goal of these letters is not to be manipulative or mean, but to express how the situation impacts you and what you have had to experience. This can be very powerful healing of the heart and soul.

CHAPTER 11

Forgiveness – Letting Go And Grieving The Loss

When we figure out why life brought us to this stage, one of our first reactions is to identify who else is responsible for getting us here. Identifying the circumstances and realizing your role in your current situation will be important parts of your journey. This has been the hardest part of the therapeutic process for every client with whom I have worked. I invite you to consider processing these last stages of your journey with someone who has been trained to be objective – either me or another certified therapist

Ambiguous Loss

"I feel alone in my marriage. On the surface, we are doing great. He has a great job, we own a nice home in the suburbs, and our kids are doing well in school. We socialize on weekends and are invited to parties and get-togethers quite often. I enjoy hosting and my husband is helpful when he is not working. However, I feel that we are emotionally distant. When I try to talk to him, I usually get one-word responses

like 'fine' and 'good' or 'acha'. I feel like he doesn't know anything about me. I worry that he feels the same way and that when our kids leave for college, we will have nothing left to say to each other."

When the eminent psychotherapist Dr. Pauline Boss wrote about *ambiguous loss* theory, she was initially talking about feeling grief and loss over those who may have passed on, but whose presence remains in your life to such an extent that you don't quite know how to exist without them. People who have lost very dear and close loved ones experience this kind of loss. Your feel as if your loved one was so close to you that they can't actually ever be really gone.

However, Dr. Boss went on to describe the type of loss that occurs when loved ones are physically present in your life, but not emotionally present. This type of loss can be absolutely devastating, and is not limited to feeling lonely in your marriage. Many of my clients taking care of a child with special needs, or of a parent with long-term illness such as Parkinson's or Alzheimer's, also feel the same way. These are forms of ambiguous loss, too – the loss of a dream or a picture you had in your mind of how your relationship with that person would be.

Your dream for this lost relationship must be both honored and grieved. Whether it was a dream to become a doctor, or to have a traditional family, or a healthy child, you now have to sit with that lost dream. Process fully what it meant for you, and how it shaped the person that you are now. More importantly, you need to discover how that unfulfilled dream has impacted your life. You can do that by following the steps below.

Grieving and Honoring the Past
Assessing the Damage

> *"I feel so much shame. I lived a life where I hurt so many. I wish I had known why that was, and then maybe my relationships would not have suffered so much. Many years ago, when an old friend told me as a joke that I seem bi-polar, I got really mad and left. I wish I had investigated what that meant. When I used to try to convince my family about the grand plans I had for what I was going to do with life and they resisted, I would come up with so many reasons in my manipulation to convince them. I was on a high and everything was going to be great. It was all going to magically happen, and everything would be fine. I would lie and keep the drama going, then get mad at loved ones and friends for not listening and doing what I said. I stayed up all night planning, absorbed in my obsession.*
>
> *Things would go well and then the dreaded 'down' feeling would creep in. I started withdrawing and getting careless and aloof. The energy and excitement vanished and the negativity, blaming, and toxic behavior would come out. So many times, my family lied for me, covered for me. So many beautiful relationships abandoned me because they couldn't deal with*

the two people they had to be with when they were with me. I feel alone. I feel like going to each and every one of the people I disappointed and telling them that I didn't know I had this painful illness! Now I know how to manage it. But why should they believe me? I broke their trust on so many levels. This is how it will be. I will be alone forever."

The above narrative shows a deep understanding of how this person has contributed to damaging his relationships. Your realization may not be this overwhelming or profound, but you do need to take stock of where you are right now. This is yet another important step in your healing journey. The anxiety you feel about righting the things you have done wrong, or the shame and guilt you feel about what you may have done to hurt yourself and others, must be honored and processed. You may have compromised elements of yourself in order to please others in your family (such as parents or a spouse). Perhaps you did this to keep the peace, or to maintain your image. Regardless of the reason, those compromised elements need attention and re-assessment.

Letting Go – Blame, Anger, and Resentment

"I am so angry at my parents. They ruined my life. Why did they even bring me into this world if all they wanted to do was control me and make me the puppet of their dreams? It's like I wasn't allowed to be a person. Everything I did or said had something to do with them, like I was a body part of

theirs with legs of my own. I know they meant well on some level, but I hate them so intensely sometimes."

"I have so much resentment for her. I feel used. It was all about her – she wanted a house, and then a better car, and then one thing or another, so we would look like we were at the same status as the fake people we socialized with. They are not our friends and couldn't care less if we got divorced. It is like nothing I could have done was enough. I faced constant comparisons with other husbands. It was like we were in a movie she had seen about marriage and if I was out of character, she was mad. She's realized it finally and is responding now, but I'm so resentful, and I feel nothing for her."

Anger is a normal emotion and is sometimes necessary and appropriate. We frequently feel angry if we feel wronged, are treated unfairly, or when things don't go as we expected they would. Anger is also a protective mechanism, because it allows us to exert some sense of control in dangerous situations.

Typically, resentments develop when that anger sits for a long time. The intensity of the original anger may lessen, but the negative feelings towards that person or event still lives inside of us. It feels like we hold onto resentment because the original event that made us angry is just too hard to accept, digest, or move on from. A lot of times, we can feel this in our body, as a form of stress.

The sad part about these feelings is that most of the time, the person we hurt most is ourselves. The amount of time your mind spends feeling that resentment, or obsessively thinking about the person who hurt you, quite literally makes you a hostage to those people and events. Re-running these thoughts and feelings in your head gives them a much longer lifespan than they deserve. In addition, be aware that many cognitive distortions develop from the negative space that long term resentment and anger create. These irrational thoughts actually can seep into the rest of your life and impact your other relationships. It is imperative that you honor your feelings and start working on letting go of anger and resentment.

But how is that even possible?

Letting Go – Forgiveness

Letting go is a powerful tool that is often underutilized. For many of us, the resistance to letting go of our past hurt comes from thinking that we are letting the other person get away with their awful behavior. Perhaps we think that we have to feel some special way when we forgive, or that we have to say those words directly to the person and then include them in our lives – but in reality, forgiveness does not mean pretending that the incident(s) or violation(s) never happened. So, what does it mean, then?

By forgiving, you move on with your grace and dignity intact. You do this by acknowledging what happened in a realistic way, both the event itself as well as its impact on you. When you forgive, you step outside your pain and consider the limitations of the person who hurt you. Sometimes this is a painful process in and of itself. Many times, forgiving has to be done over and over again. Despite the hard work that it takes, I promise you that eventually the relief you can get from forgiveness is real.

"She was a bully growing up. She shamed me about everything, even things that were not true. She said them with so much confidence that I believed her. When she made fun of my nose and said that I was ugly and fat, it became my identity. She humiliated and insulted me, and if someone complimented me in her presence, then her negative attack later on would be worse. I regretted every time I trusted her and wanted her to make amends because she always violated that trust. I feel I have forgiven her mainly because I just need to move on. She still triggers me, though. To this day, at times, all that pain comes up and I have to deal with it again."

Studies have shown that forgiveness has a positive effect on both our mental and physical well-being. When you are ready to let go of your anger, you emotionally free up space in your mind. In some people this actually feels like a weight has been lifted from them! The empty space you generate can then be filled with more positive feelings. But the most important thing to remember about forgiveness is that it is a liberating act

– the act of freeing yourself from being hostage to negative, sometimes toxic feelings.

Processing letting go with your therapist, or writing an impact letter to the person you want to forgive, are two important ways to start the healing process. (Just remember that your impact letters are just for you, and not meant to be sent. Some people like to shred or burn them after they have been written.) A key to this process is learning to create healthier boundaries for yourself. In this way, you minimize the possibility of re-experiencing the kind of situations that generated your anger in the first place.

What Needs to Change?

While on this path to change and eventual healing, it is important to remember that all of us (if not most of us) are works in progress! The more self-aware I become, the more the list of things I want to change about myself gets larger (instead of smaller). This doesn't mean I'm not improving as a person. It just means that I am developing deeper insight on what I need to change about myself, depending on where I am in my journey. Let me explain by talking about a struggle I have had for the last twenty years: trying to manage my weight and become more physically healthy.

For as long as I can remember, I struggled with weight. I was the "chubby" girl and then the pretty girl. Over and over, I heard, "if only she lost weight, she would be perfect." Starting in puberty, this was the pain I carried. It was not until I learned about SMART™ goals that I finally began to make sense of my struggles. Let me explain.

Saying that "I want to lose fifty pounds" is as terrible a goal as saying that you want "to be a better person" or "to feel happy". These goals are not realistic, or measureable. They are too big to be able to make any real progress with them.

SMART™ objectives (goals) were originally developed as a program management tool, but they have been so useful in so many applications that you now see them everywhere. Two areas where they have been particularly helpful are in time management and health behavior modification. The acronym SMART™ stands for: Specific, Measureable, Actionable, Realistic, and Time-constrained. How does that work for goal-setting?

If you stop and think about it, any really good goal has to be truly achievable. What makes a goal truly achievable?

It needs to be specific enough so that you know exactly what you need to do.

It needs to be measureable, so that you are sure that you did it!

It needs to be actionable, meaning that there are actions within your control that can be done to make the goal happen. (I'd like to be 20 years younger, but there is nothing I can do in this universe that will make that happen. Being 20 years younger is not an actionable goal!)

It needs to be <u>realistic</u> – because otherwise, why bother? Please note that a major aspect of this component is relevance, because the goal has to really mean something to you and those close to you. Your goal has to be anchored in your life and in what's possible for you. If you can't afford to join a gym right now, then planning on joining a gym eventually isn't a goal, it's a fantasy. It's not relevant to your life at this point. Put that goal on a long-term list, and go back to one that is more relevant to you for the short-term. (Maybe go over to your neighbor's three times a week to use her stair-stepper, instead?)

And the goal needs to have a <u>time</u> deadline assigned to it, because without a time deadline it isn't a goal; it's just a vague hope!

SMART™ goals are your key to bringing about the change you want in your life, because they very specifically set you up for success in whatever change you are trying to make. As you set your goals for personal change, whatever they may be, make sure that your goals are SMART™. Goals have to be achievable in order for you to give yourself a fighting chance of getting where you want to go.

So how have SMART™ goals worked for me? Let me give you some detailed examples from my personal journeys in weight loss and health and behavioral changes. I finally realized that when I wanted to lose 50 pounds, I did reach that goal a couple of times but I was not able to sustain the weight loss. So finally, after my son was born, I kept repeating in my head that I want to fire food as my therapist. I was finally addressing emotional eating. My smart goal became 'I will make deliberate healthy choices in my eating and physical activity at least 3 times a week.' I continued adding more specific, smaller goals and finally after almost 2 years I started seeing results. I still have a long way to go but now I know what I need to do.

So, as you have seen, goals need to be <u>highly</u> specific in their focus. Saying "I want to lose ten pounds" may seem specific, but my goal must meet our other requirements in order to give me the highest chance of succeeding with it. We will work on goals again a couple of chapters from now. I've given you a lot of information in the current chapter. Sit with it for now, and remember: you get to reward yourself when you do achieve your goals!

(Source: SMART Goals have been written about by multiple authors since the 1980s. Please search the internet for the model you may prefer to use in your work)

CHAPTER 12

Re-Purposing Your Story And Freedom From The Conflict

"I feel free. I know I have a lot of work to do but I feel like I will get there. The journey is so much more meaningful now. I am taking it one day at a time – even just one relationship at time, and not feeling the urgency, but rather the importance to keep changing, growing, and strengthening. This is my journey. I'm living in the now."

If you are reading this chapter, I want to congratulate you! Congratulations for being kind to yourself by taking the time to sit with your feelings. Congratulations for noticing and honoring what issues bothered you. I want to validate you for working to achieve more insight than you had at the beginning of this journey. Now you can make major progress in untangling your issues, and finding out where you are within the space of yourself and your relationships.

New Perspective on Life

This chapter focuses on the possibility of a new or refreshed perspective on self, relationships, and life. Starting today, how do you want to live differently? We touched on goals in the last chapter, but I want to slow you down on those for right now. We will not be setting goals until the next couple of chapters, when you will look at all elements of your life together and observe where you see pain and challenges, or something needs fixing.

You can develop the template for writing yourself a new story; an upgraded, or more enriched one. In this new story you will have healthy boundaries that can sustain both a healthy sense of self, <u>and</u> a healthy sense of relationships. Below is a narrative that talks about the pain that ensues when we don't have the sense of healthy boundaries in our lives.

"Our daughter is always telling us, "I have no money!" She runs out of money to pay tuition for her kids. She is in such a plight all the time. She says she will do things, like leave our home, when she finally gets her child support check, because her ex is so far behind. We try to help as much as possible. We bought her an apartment, then we started helping with her children's tuition and groceries, and a utility bill here and there. She cries about her situation and sometimes shows us so much gratitude for helping her. It is so frustrating that she throws us under the bus, then, later when she doesn't get what she wants. It's all about her – she's tired, she's sick, she's

not sleeping well at night, and she's suffering one way or another. When she visits us from out of town, she portrays herself as such a great mother and a victim of her situation. But we know she has a stellar wardrobe and a monthly billing with the salon where she gets her beauty treatments! Yet when it comes to spending on her children's education, she says she doesn't have enough. We are more than tired of helping her."

In their work with children, American psychologists Dr. Henry Cloud and Dr. John Townsend researched what it means to have healthy boundaries, and lucky for us, their work applies to adults, as well. Boundaries are especially important to those of us of South Asian heritage, specifically because our culture does not have a well-defined sense of what they are or what their value is. The lack of this concept means that it is even harder for us to develop and sustain healthy boundaries in our lives. Boundary clarifications are an essential part of personal growth and maturity. And while physical boundaries are easy to identify, emotional and psychological ones are harder to pinpoint. Families frequently tend to be "all up in each other's space", because without boundaries we can't define where we end and another person begins. But news flash: boundaries also define where one person's <u>responsibility</u> ends and where the next person's responsibility begins!

Our character greatly impacts how we do in life and whether we will thrive or struggle. Our character includes our ability or inability to do things, how responsible we are, and how we function in relationships. If we are able to solve problems and learn from failure, then this becomes a strength in our character.

Character development starts in the early years. A boy in the South Asian culture could be used to having his mom take extra care of him throughout his formative years. He may get very used to the breakfast in bed and the special teas and the head massages, and when he grows up, he may expect the same from his wife. If his wife grew up in a different type of household, or believes that you need to take care of your own self when you are sick, he may be extremely disappointed in her. Character will play a role here to see how he ultimately responds to this situation. Will he feel that his wife doesn't love him, and say mean things to her? Or will he adjust, and learn to assertively communicate that he likes a little bit of pampering when he is ill – maybe even laugh and make a joke about himself with his wife? In other words, will he develop healthy boundaries in his adult relationship, or will he stay stuck with his childish views? Each of these options say something about his character and maturity level.

Try to understand what your challenges are in developing a more mature character with healthy boundaries. Are these challenges within yourself, or within your relationships? Do you have confusion around a cultural value that you are unsure about? Does your loyalty to this value or behavior make you less committed to your heritage? What does the adult within you need in order to have healthy limits around you? Let's talk more about that.

New Narratives

Embracing your bi-cultural identity is part of the overall healing process as you untangle the personal and relational issues you may have. The process of getting comfortable with your new host culture is called *acculturation*. Acculturation occurs to varying degrees, and is one way that we shape our new narrative. Certain elements of the new culture are adopted immediately in order to make the new life possible (such as the protocol for the adults' work environment or for the kids' school system). Other elements of the new life evolve and settle in over time. A key feature of acculturation is that the family that socializes more with the new host culture tends to acculturate more quickly than the family that tends to socialize with people of their own heritage.

Here's an example. Two children of South Asian heritage both go to the same school, and are in the same grade. Ana's parents are working professionals who socialize with many American families, in addition to socializing with South Asians. They host at home, and both parents have individual friendships with colleagues and parents from the host culture. In contrast, Sarah's parents are working professionals, but their social life is limited to the temple. They do not host at home and are more introverted, with limited friendships. Sarah's parents don't like her socializing with non-South Asians, so as a result her options for making friends are more limited. Ana doesn't have this issue, and quickly forms a wider group of friends than Sarah. By the default of how her parents behave socially, Ana has become more acculturated than Sarah.

There are so many elements to our bi-cultural identity because we have both a home country and a host country. They both shape who we are, and more importantly, who we aspire to be. Early on, we realize what attributes are appreciated by others in our new society, and most of us attempt to acquire those attributes. This is a normal part of acculturation, but it can be the source of a great deal of stress. Many of us work hard to achieve appreciation, to get the "good stuff" and attract attention – but the values of our host country are not the same as the values of our home country, and these often come into conflict

Both teens and adults develop definitions of success and failure, and even our political views, based on the desire to acculturate or conform to the group we aspire to be like. At this point, I would like you to think about the people in both of your cultures that you aspire to be like. What are the attributes you value about these people or families? How could you be more like them, or handle life like they do?

Dr. Sheeza Mohsin

Cultural Competence and the New Narrative

In the context of this book, *cultural competence* is the ability to function effectively in your new host culture, moving back and forth between it and your home culture. Developing cultural competence is an integral part of feeling a sense of belonging, while still maintaining your unique identity. Resilience is a big part of this competence. Showing the skill of flexibility, which allows us to bounce back from a rough space, should become a part of our narrative – and we should be mindful to practice it daily.

I always say, if you live in snow, you better be friends with Eskimos! Learning from your host culture's experts on best practices and life in general is a smart move. It does <u>not</u> mean that you are abandoning your culture. Having friends, comfortable relationships, and a sense of community with your neighbors, other school moms, and your yoga class members only strengthens your comfort level and ability to be resilient in your new life. If you don't feel like you have that yet, then jot it down as a goal to go on the SMART™ worksheet we will be working on here in a few minutes.

"When my son came home and I gave him a snack, he asked me why I was different. I laughed in my head, thinking you are not looking in the mirror because you look just like me. When I asked him what he meant, he said that he does not see me at school like all the other moms, who are volunteering. He said they use such kind words and I 'never'

do that. They are so nice, and I sound mean. It shattered me and I was so mad at him then for saying that. But looking back, I feel grateful. I pushed myself to volunteer and through that, I made a friend. Becky was a life-saver! I feel like I hit the jackpot because I learned just by observing her. I noticed how she talked to her kids. I started saying things like, 'that's not nice' to my son, instead of 'shut up.' I feel so lucky that I have my school mom group. I feel I have learned something new each time I meet with them. My husband learns things from work, but I work inside the home. My outlet is these women. My 'school' is these women. I am so grateful."

This Is Our Home, Too

I hear a lot of South Asian families talk about going "home." It is an interesting concept, as it describes their sense of still belonging to the home culture. The most amusing element of this notion is that when families do go visit "home" (in this case, Pakistan, India or Bangladesh) they find themselves saying, "It is time to go home" when they talk about going back to the U.S. or Canada. I have done the same thing!

At this point I must acknowledge those people who have experienced adverse treatment by the host culture in the form of prejudice or discrimination. Yes, those are real and painful things! And those experiences definitely intensify the motivation to "go home" for many. But I will invite you here to make sure that you get professional help (either from me or from someone else) so that you can talk through and resolve some of your issues with these types of experiences. The reason is that being overly concerned about prejudice and discrimination can instill fear and irrational thoughts in your mind. These eventually can impact you in a negative way. An example of that is generalizing that all people of a certain group are bad because the person who has been mean to you was from that group. The truth of the matter is that every group of people whether it is a race, ethnicity or culture, includes bad and good people. Negative beliefs in those circumstances perpetuate or encourage negative behavior which is not good for any community or society.

Healthier Relationships

"I feel so much better after realizing where I am in the spectrum of this bi-cultural identity. I feel like this clarity is helping me accept who I am, instead of thinking I am not 'desi enough' or not 'American enough.' I am me. I am a socially liberal person with moderate religious values. I don't drink, but love my friends who do, and I don't judge them for it. In fact, it's liberating to enjoy them instead of judging them. They are not my clones, but are individuals who live the way that works for them. The key is to have a strong character. I feel that is the common ground for us. We have the same worries – about jobs, kids, and safety. We have the same love for shows and food. They love Indian food, and I love eating butternut squash the way it's made here because it doesn't activate my acidity the way our spices do. We even complain

about the same elements of our messy and absent-minded husbands. I am now accepting things about myself. It is okay – I'm okay. I'm enough."

Below are some questions that I would like you to answer to help you get clarity about what you want to focus on accepting about yourself. This is an important exercise to do before you go trying to change situations and relationships in your life. It is important to continue to appreciate and accept those aspects of your life in which you are thriving and doing well!

Once you have an idea of what you need to preserve, it will be easier to identify what you need to change. Write your answers down and keep track of them. Be as open and honest as you possibly can. This exercise can be a great avenue for personal growth, and can increase your understanding of the significant relationships in your life.

New Narrative for Relationships with Parents and In-Laws

- Identify different relationship dynamics you have with both your parents and your in-laws.
- What are some elements of your relationship with your <u>parents</u> that you really like, enjoy, and cherish?
- What is missing that you desire or crave from this relationship?

- Where are opportunities for you to create healthy boundaries?
- What are some elements of your relationship with your <u>in-laws</u> that you really like, enjoy, and cherish?
- What is missing that you desire or crave from this relationship?
- Where are opportunities for you to create healthy boundaries?

New Narrative for Relationships with Siblings

- What are some elements of your relationship with your <u>siblings</u> that you really like, enjoy, and cherish?
- What is missing that you desire or crave from this relationship?
- Where are opportunities for you to create healthy boundaries?

New Narrative for Relationships with Spouse and Partner

- What are some elements of my relationship with my parents that I really like, enjoy and cherish?
- What is missing that I desire or crave from this relationship?
- Where are opportunities for me to create healthy boundaries?

New Narrative for Relationships with Children

- What are some elements of my relationship with my parents that you really like, enjoy, and cherish?
- What is missing that you desire or crave from this relationship?
- Where are opportunities for you to create healthy boundaries?

New Narrative for Relationships with Friends – Bi-Cultural Values

- What are some elements of your relationship with your friends that you really like, enjoy, and cherish?
- What is missing that you desire or crave from this relationship?
- Where are opportunities for you to create healthy boundaries?

I am excited for you as you start planting seeds of new narratives, and possibly healthier relationships in your life that you will ultimately give you more fulfilling experiences in your own life and within those relationships.

STAGE THREE

Strengthening ...Always And Forever

CHAPTER 13

Introduction To Stage Three – Strengthen And Thrive

'The secret of change is to focus all your energy NOT on fighting the old, but on building the new.'

— Socrates

"I fear that as I'm doing this work and feeling better than ever, that everything will fall apart. My mom came in and said I'm not giving enough time to my family and home. She said that I'm not visiting them often enough and I'm just busy with 'friends' - like I'm taking drugs or something! The guilt is overwhelming. At least now I see it; before I just felt bad and didn't know why. She got offended because I didn't eat the biryani she made. I asked her to make it with cauliflower rice because I'm trying to avoid flour, grains, and sugar. It landed on deaf years, and yet she has been the single biggest source of my shame about my weight for my whole life.

Changing my lifestyle has been good, but confusing. People around me like things just the way they are; they get in my way and don't want me to change. These people love me, I know, but I've evolved – I say no to going out on the weekends sometimes, and sometimes I don't want go to an expensive restaurant. They order tons of food I won't eat, but I still have to pay for it because we split the bill. I'm told I'm not making an effort with them.

But I'm making an effort with me, and I'm happy in this new space."

What to Expect in This Stage?

Changing your environment's energy so that it nurtures your growth is a lot harder than changing yourself. Many times, some of the reasons we are stuck in this space is because we exist in an environment that feeds off of the energy we exuded before. You have limited time and energy. Changing even simple things about our life can be rewarding, but it can also be extremely hard for the people around us. When you were "the hostess with the mostest", and known for welcoming people to come visit anytime, but now you have reduced doing so to a quarter of what you used to do - your world will not ignore it! They may be suspicious that you are upset or offended, or that you have found other friends (who might even be of higher status!) All sorts of judgments may start flying around you.

It is important to draw a boundary so that you are not responsible for managing other people's distorted thinking. Let go of that expectation, and realize that at any given time you may make someone mad for not attending to them as they'd like, for choosing something else over them, or for preferring not to spend time, money, or even food on them. That is okay! It is crucially important for you to let go of the urge to always please others. Always pleasing others is not possible. Focus on having time for your healthier lifestyle, instead.

What Will Help You?

At this point you are probably already changing, and others are already noticing. To continue strengthening your new sense of self, you need support from those around you. I recommend making a list of people whom you consider close (or moderately close) connections. Start to share your journey toward a better lifestyle and new priorities with them. No, I am not asking you to share your therapeutic experience with them! Just share some of those things that you feel you need support with for improving. As an example, now that I am committed to eating healthy most of the time, I have started sharing this with dear friends, who will then make accommodations if they can, about my nutrition, or not be offended if I eat first and come by afterwards.

At this point, some of your friends might feel abandoned and may need to hear that it's not about them, it's about you. This is important, because if your friends translate your behavior change as arrogance, or think you're not a fun person to hang out with anymore, then you may feel pressure to separate, too soon, from your new identity. This can potentially weaken your resolve to change and interfere with your success.

As you strengthen in your new sense of self, it will be natural to need to need to work out issues with your core support group (your "tribe"). This group would include, for example, anyone you usually see at least once a week, like co-workers who you no longer go to lunch with now. You may be trying to save money or make healthier choices, or perhaps you are working out on your lunch break. Maybe you are using your lunch time three days a week to catch up with an old friend whom you have missed. It's your time to use as you see fit, and you are feeling good about these changes, so let your old friends know your plans – you can alleviate a lot of tension by being intentional with them about these changes in advance.

What May Get in Your Way?

Sometimes, as we change, we start becoming attracted to the idea of perfection. We think that we have to do every last thing that we committed to doing, and that it is an all or nothing situation. Either we do everything we planned, or we have failed! This is a kind of cognitive distortion (remember those?) that does not allow for the flexibility and malleability that life requires. There will be days or weeks when you will not be able to spend time with your kids like you originally committed to do, or to go to the water aerobics you have grown to love participating in. It's also okay if you ate a few bites of the dessert you just couldn't resist, or if you slept in and did not work out first thing on Thursday morning. Once in a while it is even alright if you were not able to visit your parents or call your mom. You did it all those other times! Forgiveness is a part of flexibility. As I have discussed elsewhere in this book, forgiveness is not just for others – it is for yourself too. You are still doing well.

In quality improvement (a form of management science) I like recommending the 80:20 rule. If you are good 80% of the time and not as good 20% of the time, you are still in a good spot and are improving.

How to Be Kind to Yourself in This Stage of Work

Notice the fine things in your life, such as the remarkable effort you make in changing how you live your life every day. Consider how creative you have become in how you utilize your time, spend your money, and eat more nutritious meals. Observe how regularly you are physically active, as well as how much more socially active you are in relationships that lift your spirits. You no longer participate in relationships that bring you down. Notice the calmness you feel now when you work and spend time doing activities that bring you joy, instead of what brings you anxiety and misery. Take time to celebrate your efforts!

Recommendations for Self-Care

Now that we are in stage three, I recommend starting to engage in mindfulness exercises. Mindfulness involves focusing on being extremely aware of what you sense and feel in the moment, without judging anything, and without feeling any negative emotions. This can be harder than it sounds! Deep breathing and guided imagery are some variations of mindfulness activities that may help you reduce stress and feel more relaxed.

Notice where you feel strain in your body when you are doing these activities. Your body will tell you what it needs. Mindfulness is actually a simple type of meditation that can help you improve your concentration and quality of sleep. It has even been proven in some cases to help reduce symptoms of stress, anxiety, and pain from various health conditions.

CHAPTER 14

Generating New Goals For Yourself And Your Relationships

"The significant problems we face cannot be solved by the same level of thinking that created them."

– Stephen Covey, First Things First

As you read over the narratives that follow, take a moment to reflect on the disconnect between how we spend our time and what is really important to us.

"There are so many things I want to do. I know I have to do them, but I never seem to get to them. I make lists all the time. I feel I have no control over my time. In any particular day, things pop up and I have to respond to them. Like yesterday, I was going to organize my closet, but my daughter called from school saying she left her music sheets on her bed. I had to run and get those to her. When I went there, my friend bumped into me and shared that she needs to go to the doctor because her baby isn't doing well, and she doesn't want to take her older child along. Of course, I understand how hard juggling that is, so I took her kid home. Between

calls from mom and my sister and taking care of this kiddo, I don't know where the time went. And then the bell rang, and my daughter came home from school. No closet organizing, no healthy cooking and no workout. I feel so bad."

"I know I've had long hours at work historically. By the time I would get home, my wife would be done with dinner and homework, and the kids would be in bed. During the weekends, we had so many social plans, the kids had birthdays and activities to attend, and then we had family gatherings. I don't know where the time went. Now I am father to these teenagers who don't have much to say to me. I am so eager to get to know them and spend time with them and discuss current affairs with them, but we have no relationship. All I get is monosyllabic responses, like 'yes,' 'okay,' and 'fine.' The other day, I saw them hanging with my younger brother. He would always come once a week to hang out with them, regardless of what was going on, sometimes just for fifteen minutes. I think they like him more than me."

A lot of the material in this chapter is rooted in Mr. Stephen Covey's book, *First Things First*. Covey is an American businessman and inspirational speaker known for his time and organizational management self-help books. When I read his book for the first time back in the 1990s, I felt a shift in my worldview and thinking. I felt that I had found a touchstone that showed me my goals were achievable, as long as certain aspects of them were clear.

Earlier, I spoke to you about my chronic inability to lose weight and sustain the loss. This battle had taught me many things about the problems we meet in trying to achieve difficult goals. The process of attempting to set goals, making them SMART™ goals, and then working to achieve them is an intense experience. We may just give up if we are not kind to ourselves along the way. We have to wholeheartedly embrace being mindful enough to truly spend the time doing what's important to us.

This is the problem that Covey explains so well in his books! If you have to put off your workout, family time, a visit to your parents' home, work, a special project, or something else pressing that you really should do, then you may have an *urgency addiction*. Urgency addiction seems pretty self-explanatory, but it can be more complex than it might seem at first. If you are addicted to urgency, then you feel the need to repeat smaller tasks over and over, such as clean out your inbox, or check your social media. That seems like you are getting work done, but in reality, you are using those repetitive tasks as a "time suck" to keep yourself from tackling bigger, more important jobs - until the urgency gets so extreme that you <u>must</u> make yourself do it.

So, urgency addiction is actually a form of procrastination. "I can't work on that project now – I have to answer these emails first!" Urgency addiction is a self-destructive behavior that causes you unnecessary anxiety, and prevents you from having the time you need to function truly effectively. It works, but at a cost. If this sounds like you, start trying to limit your urgency addiction "time suck" tasks now.

SMART™ Goals

Now that you understand much more about time management and the obstacles to personal change that you may encounter, start thinking about some SMART™ goals you want to achieve. Let's work through one example to show you how it's done. For example, let's say you want to "get healthier". Remember that a SMART™ goal needs to be specific, measureable, actionable, realistic, and time-constrained. So certainly, saying, "I will stop drinking soda" is more specific than, "I will get healthier". But is that enough to help you achieve it? Your goal also needs to be measureable. How about "I will stop drinking soda during the week"? That is certainly measureable, because you will know for sure when you are doing it. We're getting better here!

Additionally, your goal needs to be actionable. In other words, it needs to be descriptive, such as, "I will stop drinking soda during the week after 2 pm". This is becoming a very good example of a goal! But what about how realistic it is? Can you really do this every day at work? Instead, how about saying, "I will stop drinking soda during the week after 5 pm"? That way if you need an energy burst late in the day at work, you can still have it. And finally, your goal needs to be time-constrained.

Let's say, "For the next two weeks, I will stop drinking soda during the week after 5 pm." Looking back, aren't you much more likely to be successful doing that than you are to just "get healthier"?

This is how SMART™ goals help set you up for success. Start small, be successful, and work your way up to larger goals. And remember I said to be sure to celebrate your successes!

Our Various Roles and Relationships

I talk about having balance in life among all the dimensions of wellness shown on the wellness wheel (spiritual, emotional, physical, etc.) - but we all have so many different roles we must fulfill, how will we ever manage that? Balancing our needs for wellness with the competing demands that our roles require from us is yet another dance in life.

Here's a great secret I've been waiting to tell you: One of the best ways we can help to generate this balance is to create goals for each of our various roles. You are getting to be an expert at goals by now! For each of your different roles in life, create goals that will allow you to make time to be present in your relationships with others. Using goal-setting to make time for these vital relationships is crucial way to cultivate contentment in your life. And don't forget that you also have a relationship with yourself! The 'Self' is also an important person to recognize, and this is where self-care comes into play.

One of our most crucial roles is that of a parent, and the following are examples of goals that you could create in order to prioritize the important things in your relationships that revolve around that role.

"For the next year I will spend 15 minutes every weeknight reading to my son from a book that he chooses, even if it is the same book over and over." (Check up on me – is this SMART™? Maybe it could be more realistic!)

"For the rest of this month, on the weekdays that my daughters go to dance class, I will engage them in conversation afterwards on the ride home, instead of tuning them out and listening to my iPod."

Guiding Principles of Goal Setting

It is character building to take other people's interests into account when making goals. Unfortunately, many people create goals that are socially or financially motivated, and do not attempt to balance these goals with the other aspects of a healthy life. Focusing on money or social advancement usually generates feelings of emptiness, because they are goals that can rarely be sufficiently satisfied. Think of a family that wants to become wealthy. If their goal isn't pursued with an eye to balancing out other relationships in life, then, even though they may have success, it may be at the cost of compromising their physical, emotional, or spiritual health.

Principles are the anchors, or the personal compass, that give a person the direction he or she needs to point them forward. Principles are usually timeless, and classic examples are fairness, equity, honesty, and trust. They regulate our decisions to act even when no one is watching. If we are aware of our principles, and keep them in mind when we set our goals, then we are more likely to maintain an overall sense of balance among all of our roles and relationships. This is how we maintain a healthy and fulfilling life.

It is important to understand what principles and values we are anchored to and how they are serving us. For example, identifying the top 4 or 5 relationships and roles we have in life help us prioritize how we have to divide our available time among those relationships.

"The key is not to prioritize what's on your schedule, but to schedule your priorities."

– Steven Covey

Your 10 Daily List for Healthy Self and Relationships

Having a customized list of 10 daily habits and behaviors that can strengthen your character and make you feel like you experienced a wholesome day. Why? Because you are spending time doing the things that are most important to you! (Please note that these habits do not have to be strenuous.) For example, here is my list for this year:

1. Move every day for at least twenty minutes or more (this way when I cannot exercise or go to the gym, I am at least on my feet cleaning and organizing. I don't walk my dog, but you could).

2. Show my kids love and laugh with my kids about something and hug them every day. It's a must

3. Spend at least twenty minutes of focused time with each kid five days a week. Listen, but don't advise.

4. Plan to eat healthy five times a week.

5. Think about family and call one family member daily.

6. Tidy up the home as a shared responsibility with the kids for 10-15 minutes daily. Enjoy my environment.

7. Spend 30 minutes of guilt free time in an indulgence like TV or Social Media.

8. Spend a few minutes daily on Prayer and gratitude.

9. Work hard to sharpen my skills with effort (yes daily) and stay committed to thinking about my clients and what could help them.

10. Enjoy my chai or drive time with a favorite friend or family member every day (they message to find out when I'm driving or having chai. Then we catch up).

Note: I update and modify it as soon as I realize something is not working. Remember the list is made to serve you, not the other way around. If it is not serving you well, change it

Good Luck making yours!

CHAPTER 15

Movement Between The Steps And Stages

""Life is what happens to you while you're busy making other plans."

— John Lennon.

Your experience of reading this book has not been a linear journey, even if you read the book straight through without jumping around from one chapter to another. That is because personal growth is never a straightforward process. Even though you read about the steps in a certain order, your brain doesn't process them as a rigid sequence. You experienced different parts of the book in different frames of mind. You may have encountered an idea you weren't yet ready to apply, or an issue you couldn't quite untangle yet. But the next time you picked up the book, suddenly that issue seemed much clearer, and you could see a way through your confusion in order to deal with it. As you progressed, you found meaning and clarity in your relationship issues that you just hadn't been able to see earlier on.

It's like learning how to drive a car in a beautiful neighborhood. Yes, initially you have to know the basics of driving the car, but after that first initial fearfulness passes, you begin to relax and notice different things around you. Then true joy comes from seeing how much you improve every day – and finally, you become an expert driver. In the same way, you have wandered back and forth using various techniques and information you have learned in this book. Now you are at the point of mastering the re-invention of your new life. You have more competence and awareness than ever before, so now you can soak up this amazing experience to its fullest measure!

The reality is that your journey is not always going to go as planned. The only constant in life is change. Circumstances change, tragedies happen, and loved ones have problems that can impact us in ways we never could have imagined. I must remind you to be kind to yourself, to try to become more comfortable with the unknown, and to keep perfecting how you drive!

"I had so many plans for what I was going to do until I found out that life had a different plan for me - at least temporarily. After getting a cancer diagnosis, your mind just doesn't work the way it worked the day before. I'm grieving so much; I didn't realize all the emotions I had. From thinking about what will happen to my children, to resenting the unhealthy, toxic people in my life who sucked out my positive energy – they make me angry, and sad and hurt. Sometimes all the

emotions come out at the same time. It wasn't until I started practicing kindness and telling myself 'it is okay,' that things started getting better. Like other tragedies you wouldn't wish on other people, they have an amazing effect on you.

It's like mindfulness on steroids. You suddenly start looking at each hour as a gift that you need to spend doing something special, or meaningful, or purposeful. Time becomes a valuable kind of money that you have to spend carefully. When you used to tell me to treat it like that, and not worry so much about little things, it didn't sink in like it does now.

The reality is none of us know when we are going to die. We just know we will. I want to be mindful and carry on with all the great work I have done on myself. I will continue this journey until my last breath, with no regrets and with so much contentment."

Knowing the Difference

It is important to notice whether or not the goals you work on yield the results you hope for. Do you need to continue working on them now, or give them a break to work on something else? Please note that I'm not talking about the tangible, practical goals such as eating better, exercising more, going to school regularly, or working longer on a project. Instead, I'm talking about some of the less tangible emotional and spiritual goals that you have set for your self and your relationships. These types of goals are more elusive to measure and to maintain, even if you set them up as SMART™ goals. Sometimes our progress on these goals can get stuck. This will be when you may need to pause, take a break, and step out of the situation in order to gain perspective. In this way you can achieve better clarity about how you have been approaching matters, and what obstacles may have gotten in your way. An example of this type of goal might be not letting yourself be pulled into a bickering match every time your mother makes snarky comments about your new clothes.

Continue Stepping Forward…Continuously

"It was not until I was divorcing that I realized the kind of parenting I experienced growing up. We were a typical South Asian family that always reported from a 'fine' position. Looking back, I am not really angry at my parents because this is all they knew. As immigrants, they were so busy all the time - making sure that there was food on the table, that bills were paid, and that they could pursue their careers so they could get ahead in the American Dream. It was kind of like we were just left to raise ourselves. There was no malicious intent and we had nice family rituals, but noticing our emotions was simply not something they did. We were so busy appreciating their hard work that we never complained about anything. They were so visibly tired when they came home that we just hugged and made small talk. I didn't realize that I had become so loyal to pushing my feelings under the rug and not pointing out something, even when I felt bad.

I entered my marriage the same way. Voicing my needs is not something I know how to do. I was just grateful and kept going. I didn't know what was eating me up inside and making me feel bad because we were financially secure. After therapy I talked to my brothers and sister and realized each of us processed it differently. I didn't know that my brother was bullied, and my sister thought of suicide. It brought up so much for me; I felt like I was back at square one."

It is okay to go back and forth in how you feel about your progress! You will find that new feelings and memories pop up as you move through this journey, and each needs to be processed when it does. Think of it like appreciating a painting. The more time you spend with a painting, the more you will learn about it, the more closely you will look at it, the more details you will notice – and the more you will enjoy and appreciate the artistry and experience involved in creating it. So many of my clients feel that as soon as they get to a place of closure in one area of their life, something triggers them and they begin thinking about a completely different aspect of their journey. Many things can go unnoticed when you are loyal to an irrational belief or hung up on a resentment. They can prevent you from seeing a larger truth, and it is these larger truths that we must keep uncovering, repairing, and strengthening. It's a beautiful journey.

CHAPTER 16

Managing The Heart's Desire And The Mind's Resistance

Dealing with your own resistance to change and the urge to give up and go back to how things were.

"I knew what I needed to do even then. I knew I needed to speak to my wife and my children with love and consideration. I feel so much shame about my temper. I don't know what happens. It's just that when I get triggered I take off and behave in a way that is so embarrassing when I think about it later on. When my son called me out on my behavior, I was so offended I did not talk to him for days. My father used to yell at us. On some days he would get his belt out and whoever engaged with him first 'got it'. I have never hit my children. But the yelling is something I have not been able to get a handle on. It is getting better though."

"I hate these negative thoughts and this anxiety that comes up for me when my parents start asking me questions. I don't know how to be assertive with them because I don't want to be disrespectful. If I ever talk about a struggle with them, it is a party for them. My mom will call her sister, not to mention

her best friend, to discuss the heck out of my problem. Oh, and my Dad is that worst! He thinks talking about your kids' problems is something that builds community with his co-workers, since we can't talk about religion or politics. He has to throw me and my problems under the bus. Then the unsolicited advice seeps in. Random people I come across not only seem pretty well aware of the situation, but they also take it upon themselves to start giving me advice. I hate it. There is no point trying to change or be better. Let's just stay in this misery because my parents will definitely be able to engage with others about it!"

By this time you have had an opportunity to see how hard it is to change even the smallest aspects of ourselves (and others') behavior. We want to change our thoughts and actions, but we also seem to resist that change with every fiber of our being. My goal for this next to last chapter is to help you see why that resistance works the way it does. First, we must understand a few important things about the brain and how it works. No, I am not going to go all scientific on you! I will keep it simple.

Understanding How the Brain Works with Emotions

As you know, our brain is a versatile organ, a powerhouse of control for our body and for our actions. We will only discuss two parts of this amazingly complex organ. One part is in the front of your brain, and one is at the bottom. The part in the front is called the pre-frontal cortex, or PFC. It is involved in making decisions and controlling our voluntary actions, so for our purposes, I will call it the "smart" brain. The part in the bottom of the brain is called the amygdala. Because the amygdala is a part of the brain system that regulates emotion (the limbic system), I will call the amygdala the "fear" brain.

As I have said, the smart brain is responsible for our critical thinking, and for all the good decisions that we make. Being thoughtful, careful, and cautious occurs in this area, as does making plans and thinking through the consequences of our actions. Like a special vault, the smart brain also carries all the wisdom and information that we acquire. Whether it's from reading books like this, hearing podcasts and seminars, or from watching Oprah™, it all gets dumped into the smart brain. This part of the brain even works to present ourselves as favorably as possible in all of our relationships!

In contrast, the fear brain plays a very different role for us. Some researchers say that it is the reason the human race has survived as long as it has. The fear brain helps protect us from getting hurt by generating fear when we perceive danger. This fear then triggers our body's automatic defenses either to fight or run away. If we did not see a car coming, it triggers a response so that we "make a break" for it. If someone attacks us, it triggers a response so that we either run away or fight back. Sometimes, the fear brain triggers a freeze response as well, because we are trying to buy some time to figure out what to do about a situation that we perceive as a threat. It's literally a life-saving function!

But here is the interesting part, and it has always fascinated me. Whenever we are scared, thinking that something awful is about to happen, our fear brain takes over. It gives us three choices to respond: fight, flight, or freeze – that's pretty much it. Our fear brain is able to limit our choices in this way by forcing blood to flow only to it, cutting off the smart brain and preventing it from being able to function. You may have noticed that it can be very hard to make any kind of big decision when you are scared to death. As a matter of fact, all you can often do at that point is to try and handle your fear and get out of the terrifying situation. And now you know the reason why that is.

You may see where I am going with this explanation. Essentially, whenever we feel threatened, all of our wisdom, knowledge, and learning gets shut down inside the smart brain's vault, and we temporarily have no access to it. The only responses available to us are fight, flight, or freeze. This process is a great tool when we are physically threatened, such as during a natural disaster – but unfortunately our brains react to emotional threats in the same way.

Let me illustrate this with an example. When two people are in disagreement with one another, they may start the argument while utilizing their smart brains. Each party is using what they know, sharing evidence, and trying to be cordial as they navigate this uncomfortable space. And then one party says something that triggers fear. We are done using the smart brain here! The response from the other party is to attack (fight), or to walk away (flight), or to simply shut down (freeze). This inevitably makes the situation worse, and now you have a full-blown argument with yelling and screaming and all that comes with it. See how that works? These otherwise smart, rational people are now fighting, with no access to their smart brains nor all the vital diplomacy skills they have collected over their lifetime.

What is the take-home message here? When we work on relationships and sensitive situations, the key is to manage the triggering fear brain. The immediate thought once your fear brain is triggered is thinking of worst case scenario, or catastrophizing. Once we have explained to ourselves that we are just scared, we are able to access our smart brain's executive management skills. If we can keep that vault open, we have a much better chance of resolving our issue in a way that honors all the hard work we have done to better ourselves – with no ill-feeling, no screaming, no hitting, and no actions we will regret later.

Change: Stages and Resistance

Change is hard and you have probably have seen plenty of evidence for that. Whether you try to change a habit as straightforward as making yourself exercise daily, or as subtle as stopping being suspicious of your spouse, the process of initiating and sustaining change is one of the hardest things you'll ever have to do – that is, until you figure out where you are in the stages of change at which point it becomes a breeze, or close enough! Before I get into the details of how a typical change cycle happens, I want to tell you an interesting thing to notice about change. Change is usually easier when it is your own decision, rather than when someone else decides for you. For example, if you initiate a move because you got a new job, it may be an easier transition for you than it is for your spouse.

So why is that? In the late 1970s American health psychologists Dr. James Prochaska and Dr. Carlo DiClemente published a model of behavior change that makes this phenomenon very understandable. They called it the "Stages of Change", and it explains how people approach altering a negative behavior or acquiring a positive behavior. This easy to understand model is so helpful that since its publication it has been used to help people change a long list of different types of behaviors. It describes change as a series of six stages, rather than as one simple step. People can move back and forth within the stages, and can even stay stuck in one stage forever. (For example, your mother has been saying that she is going to quit smoking for the last 35 years – but it hasn't happened yet!) Each of the six stages has its own unique characteristics, and it can be immensely helpful to understand where you are among the stages when you are trying to change something about your life. Let's take a look at this remarkable model below in order to see why making and sustaining change can be so hard.

1. Pre-Contemplation

"When I suddenly lost my temper on my wife in front of my relatives during Thanksgiving holiday, my uncle and my older cousin took me out on a drive. My father had a temper when we were growing up, so I couldn't understand what the big deal was. My uncle, who is such an old-fashioned guy, told me I needed help, and that this level of anger is not normal. My brother told me he was embarrassed by my behavior because his wife was there, and his teenage daughter told him that I am an emotionally abusive husband. I was not ready for that heavy load of feedback. I was extremely defensive and kept denying it and justifying my position."

In the stage of pre-contemplation people have little to no awareness that a problem even exists. As a result, there is definitely no motivation to change. Then, as you begin to feel strong emotional reactions to feedback in your environment, you start connecting outside events to the problem behavior. You are just starting to realize that there may be an issue.

2. Contemplation

"I was so mad at my friend. When they did not invite me on their Vegas trip, I was embarrassed and felt excluded. I know I get a little out of control when I drink , but come on! We have

made some great stories on those vacations. I don't drink that often, so I'm not an alcoholic. But I do know that when I drink, I get carried away. I just need to know when to stop. I get in this funk where I feel like I need to forget all the tension in life and have a good time. They have all become boring, if you ask me, watching their limits and being healthy. Who goes to Vegas to go biking? Maybe I will go check out the therapist my friend said helped him get healthier. We'll see. I do struggle with work the next day, so maybe I should take it more seriously. It can't hurt."

This stage is one of self-re-evaluation. It involves re-thinking (and re-feeling) how you see yourself in relation to the issue or challenge that is potentially a problem for you. You will notice when you binge eat, or stay up late to binge Netflix, or avoid spending time with your family, that you are more aware of your issues than before. This is the stage where you realize that a problem exists, but the commitment to change or act differently is still weak, or non-existent.

3. Preparation

"I am hopeful. I had my free consultation with the nutrition coach, and then went to two different gyms to find out about their monthly fees. My friend who works out at one of them said I can go with her initially until I figure things out. I'm such an extrovert. The thought of seeing her there makes me feel better. I have blocked time on my calendar too, so I'm not

hiding behind my favorite excuse of not having time. I feel good about this."

During this stage, your mind gets ready for the change. Finally the buy-in to take action is stronger than the belief that change cannot be made. You will find yourself believing in your ability to change, and being committed to the process. You also will start noticing those around you who are supportive of your positive change, and those who are not. You are gathering your resources!

4. Action

"I am on a roll and I felt so good after talking to my counselor. I did not eat out more than once a week for this entire month. I only went to the coffee shop on Sunday to get a celebratory latte! I even met my goal of mindful spending – no Amazon™ deliveries or retail therapy! I kept my social media time under sixty minutes per day, and on Tuesday and Thursday I hardly used it at all because I have a dance class. I just paid off my Amex yesterday. It feels awesome! I can do this!"

This is the most emotional and enthusiastic stage, where you are actively trying to make the change at last. Here, you are "on a roll". You learn to trust and accept others' support for your change, and you replace old negative behaviors that weren't serving you well with more positive ones. You are finally at the point where you feel good about the changes, because the benefits they bring are becoming more and more visible.

5. Maintenance

"I can't believe how different life seems. It actually seems to have slowed down. After a year of working on this, I feel like things flow out of me and into my life so organically now. I'm spending time, money, and resources on the good stuff – healthy relationships, a healthy lifestyle, and most importantly, a healthy mindset. Is this really the new me? Wow! I like me a lot!"

This is an important part of the change cycle, where the new behavior replaces the old one. This is like having a good back up system, so if surprises present themselves you are ready to do some fire-fighting to get things back to functioning well. You have evolved and are enjoying this space in your life.

6. Relapse, or "Hiccups"

The Stages of Change model is a highly realistic description of how humans deal with change, and it includes a stage of relapse, or backsliding. I like to call it "hiccups". We have said all along that we can't be perfect, and the model acknowledges that here. In the relapse stage, we may fall back into our old pattern or previous behaviors. As behavior changes go, quitting smoking is notorious for its association with relapses. Addictions are tough for everyone to a greater or lesser degree.

Upward Spiral

The good news is that you can relapse but still "get back in the groove" and keep working on yourself. Learning happens with each relapse, and we have the option to use what we have learned in order to help ourselves on our next try. Hopefully we become stronger and more resilient after a relapse, and the amount of time we spend being demoralized gets shorter. We can get back into our groove and try again!

Congratulations! You have come this far. The above concepts are some of the most important to understand, so you can initiate and sustain change. The stages will help you know which stage you are in and you can get the help and support needed for that stage. When I work with my clients this is an important element I look for in their journey. Choosing techniques and interventions is easier for me when I know where they are struggling.

CHAPTER 17

Creating A Life Of Healthy Behaviors And Self-Care

'We are what we repeatedly do. Success is not an action but a habit."

— Aristotle

Maintaining Healthy Relationships

"My mom loves me a lot. I know she worries about me, which is why she needs to know where I am and what I'm doing all the time. If I don't tell her where I am or if she realizes I went somewhere she didn't know about, she gets very hurt. My girlfriend thinks that is not healthy and that I am a 35 year old man and don't need to report to my Mom all the time. I don't know how to explain my relationship with my mom to her. I wonder sometimes if she is right."

"I just don't enjoy going out anymore. Every time my husband sees me laugh with someone or talk to someone, he gets jealous and we fight on our way back home. He doesn't say it, but either that night or over the next few days, he is so mean to me and he goes out of his way to criticize me. It

makes me feel terrible. He gets really angry and tells me it is because of me that he behaves this way. When I respond, he attacks my character and makes me feel worthless. When I tell him how I feel, he says I'm too sensitive and cannot take feedback. I get so confused. It's not worth it."

"She is my best friend, but that doesn't mean that I cannot talk to other people or make other friends. The moment other people talk to me, I can sense her frowning on the side and getting mad. Later on, I'll get a long text from her about how she felt ignored and that I was not considerate of her, because I was busy socializing with others. I hate how she blows it out of proportion. I don't want to say anything because I know she is struggling, and I don't want to hurt her feelings. It's getting hard though."

A significant part of thriving in life depends upon our ability to create, grow, and sustain healthy relationships. These relationships strengthen us, and help us look forward to life and our daily interactions with others. Unhealthy relationships, however, cause anxiety because we worry about how we are going to manage them. This anxiety affects our overall wellbeing, as well as our mental health. To help you distinguish between healthy and unhealthy relationships, here are some key elements of healthy relationships.

Communicating Honestly with Kindness

Communication is healthy when you check on each other's assumptions and don't expect the other person to read your mind. There is no psychic component, even in close relationships, where the other person should telepathically know what you need or how you feel!

A lot of times South Asians misunderstand disagreement as a violation of loyalty. Our culture dictates that if you are someone's brother or friend, then you have to stand by them, regardless of whether you think they are right or wrong. This is an irrational view because no one can be right all of the time. Healthy relationships require honest, but kind, communication. One way to determine if your communication with someone is healthy, is whether or not you are given time to think before you respond to them. If instant agreement is expected, then the communication is not healthy, and neither is the relationship.

Respect – Wishes, Boundaries, Space and Everything in Between

Respect is another key component of a healthy relationship. It is important to show your family, partner, or children respect as the individuals that they truly are. This respect can be something quite basic for a child, such as respecting their wishes when they say they are full and ready to stop eating. Of course, as South Asians we know how to show love to our family through food! This is not always healthy, however, and can even trigger emotional eating disorders, such as binging or refusing food.

When a friend says they don't feel like going out because they are tired, or a sister or brother asks you to knock before you enter their room, then they are asking for basic personal respect and consideration. Respect also comes from listening to others' views without offering judgment or criticism; in this way we can truly understand their perspective. Agreeing to disagree is also a form of respect, and forms a crucial part of any healthy relationship

Knowing where you end, and others in your family and community, begin is a vital component of boundary management. We must realize that we are our own person, with our own set of beliefs, likes, and dislikes. Ours may be very different from those of the other people who live in our home, or different from the people with whom we work or go to school. They may well be of South Asian heritage, but still be different from you in many ways! Respecting your own wishes, and not getting drawn into trying to please others (even though they remain very dear to you) is yet another delicate balance you must learn to manage. Understanding where others are different from you, and where they are similar to you, helps you embrace others just as they are. It also allows you to embrace yourself. This balancing act can generate a great deal of contentment.

Trust

Trust is an integral component of healthy relationships that is somewhat related to honesty. It has its own heading here, however, because of how important it is. Trust occurs when you promise what you will do and then you actually do what you promised. Another example would be when you are the first person to let your family know that something bad has happened, so that they do not find out from a third person. Trust also means acting in not just your own, but in someone else's best interests as well, even if they are not physically present.

Mindfulness and Self-Care

Eckhart Tolle is a German philosopher/psychologist who underwent a transformative spiritual experience that appeared to have the qualities of a Buddhist enlightenment! As a result, he became a spiritual teacher, and began to write books. Living in the now, Tolle said, is key to mindfulness and success, because it allows you to make the most of your circumstances, whatever they happen to be. Without the distractions of worrying about your past and your future, you can concentrate on responding effectively to the choices you have in front of you in the present.

Following this approach means that you must also remain mindful of taking care of yourself. I cannot emphasize this enough. Adequate self-care allows you to stay healthy mentally, spiritually, and emotionally, as well as in your social relationships. You won't have the stamina for change without self-care, but first you have to remain mindful of yourself and your own needs in order to make the commitment for self-care.

So practically speaking, how do you go about including self-care in your daily routine? For me, I have to make it part of my to-do list – quite literally. On most mornings, I get up and make a task list for the day. Right alongside things like "clean the kitchen" and "call the plumber," I slot in one or more self-care tasks – every day. They are just as non-negotiable as getting the dishes done or cooking dinner.

Below you'll find my personal list of self-care ideas that I found on the internet. There were so many! I have combined a few but I think everyone should make their own list of self-care ideas to pull from daily. My list isn't one-size-fits-all. For example, I know a lot of folks might put "go for a run" or "go to the gym" on their self-care list, but those items just aren't emotionally fulfilling for me, so I left them off. However, feel free to add them to your own list. As long as you enjoy every idea you put on this list, you can also use it as a resource for choosing activities to reward yourself with when you achieve one of your SMART™ goals. Again, please remember to work hard as well. Just indulging in these and not working on yourself and your life responsibilities is not a good idea either. Enjoy!

- Sit on the porch or in your back yard – just sit
- Take a nice walk with no purpose or goal.

- Take a bubble bath, with candles and music or sit under the shower for a few minutes.
- Binge watch a show and give yourself permission to watch guilt-free.
- Watch funny videos (we do that as a family, so we can laugh together)
- Sing loudly (it does annoy my kids – a lot)
- Go for a drive on your favorite road or scenic route.
- Watch the sun rise or sun set. Don't take any pictures or post about on social media- just watch.
- Go star gazing with a friend. Take a blanket with you.
- Get a pedicure or a manicure.
- Research something that you have been interested in but have3n't had the time to dive into yet.
- Say 'no' to someone. Do it with kindness and respect.
- Take the time to do hair and makeup, for no other reason than it makes you feel great
- Edit who you follow on social media (if they don't bring you joy, they may need to go.
- Look at your list of toxic friends and start a plan to transition out of those relationships
- Have lunch with a colleague you enjoy or admire
- Pick a bouquet of fresh flowers for yourself.
- Light candles, put on music and diffuse some oils.

- Write a list of ten things you are grateful for and why
- Go to bed early or sleep in late
- Write a letter to yourself appreciating all your strengths and accomplishments
- Reward yourself after achieving a goal you set for yourself.
- Get a massage
- Go to the park and play on the playground.
- Wear an outfit that makes me feel great, even if you have no reason to.

No take a moment now and pick 5 things you may like from this list that you can consider doing at least once a week to be kind to yourself.

I am excited for you.

CHAPTER 18

What I Wish For You

"If you get the inside right, the outside will fall into place."

– Eckart Tolle

The following narratives express the thoughts and feelings of my clients who have made significant progress in their journey, and are experiencing the joy and relief that come from having done such difficult work. Let's see if they can express what you would like to feel about your life.

The Contentment of Healthy Relationships

"I was tired of chasing relationships and rescuing them to feel better. I felt exhausted trying to create this perfect family, and I feel like the one making most of the effort. What I needed to do was to rescue myself. Once I had figured this out, life was nothing but feelings of bliss and gratitude. No it isn't perfect, but I don't feel the angst, and I don't feel tangled and surrounded with toxicity. I feel calm, and whole. I can only do my part; and I am doing it! Life is good.

The Freedom of Healthy Boundaries

"I am in shock. My mom asked me to see when I would have time and availability to take care of some errands for her. 'When I have time and availability' is an alien concept for her. There was no guilt, no shame – just a question. I never thought this day would come. I cannot believe I was able to have that assertive, but respectful, conversation with her… and she listened! I placed a healthy boundary and she noticed that I'm a separate person who 'should' be focusing on her own family and not just her needs – it is remarkable. I love it!"

Living Life to Its Fullest Potential

"Life is not perfect by any means, but I am so content with it. I am doing what I should be doing. I'm mindful on levels I never thought existed for me. I feel responsible and am proud of how I am working on my responsibilities. I am not there yet, but I'm working on it and every day feels so meaningful, because I rarely have regrets about how I spend my time. I'm responsible for how I spend time; I am responsible for who I'm spending time with, and I'm responsible for my money and the end of my relationships. This is the way to be. Even though I have so much clarity on what I need to work on, I feel I have arrived."

Dr. Sheeza Mohsin

Feeling I Am Enough

"The fear of being alone is a real, scary fear that keeps many people in toxic relationships. It was my biggest fear when I divorced, but not anymore. I'm feeling good about myself and feel so relieved from letting go. I have faced my fear. Initially, I felt anxious about finding the right person because I was not filtering all of the advice I was getting: 'You'll get in the habit of being by yourself, so don't delay finding someone.' 'If you come across someone take the initiative – no need to slow down.' There were other messages that I can't even remember. I am happy to report that life is good. I have finally started noticing my worth.

I am a super amazing catch. No, I will not settle for the heck of it. What I desire is a woman who is strong enough to hold me tight when I'm falling apart and romance who I am, not the 'idea' of me in terms of lifestyle and paycheck. She will not be intimidated by my success, but will be proud of it and flaunt it, because my heart will belong to her. She will have the courage to be vulnerable, romantic, and loving. She will enjoy being around me and I will not hide myself to make her feel better. She will get amused by my energy and admire my character and get turned on thinking of how we will play in bed. I know the universe will present her and she will reach out. She will love my flaws and not be afraid. Why am I feeling that confident? Because I feel I am enough. Right now, right here. And I am so grateful that I worked on myself!"

My Wish for You…

I am so excited for you to have arrived at this stage in your journey where you are exploring ways to better yourself. Whatever the struggle was that motivated you to read this book, I hope you have greater clarity regarding why you were in that space, and some idea of where to go next. Emotional wellness, and investing in strengthening your mind, can be one of the most valuable uses of your resources. You have already taken the first step by buying this book. Keep moving forward in your journey. I would like to leave you with my top ten reasons why you should continue your journey of self-discovery and self-improvement into the future, either through visiting a therapist, or through exploring the resources I have included at the end of this book.

10 inspirations to pay attention to yourself:

This is a limited list of wisdom I have collected from sources around me.

1. Life goes by fast. Don't waste time watching others live it.

2. We train other people how to treat us. Start training them better.

3. Words are like airplanes; they take you places. When Dr. Jennings would say this, it was almost annoying. Now it makes sense. Words design our future. Be

mindful as you organize them in your life. We get loyal to the wrong ones sometimes.

4. At the end of the day; your resentments and regrets can rent more space in your mind than your gratitude and hopes. Focus on the good stuff increases its presence in your life.

5. Get busy living or get busy dying - From one of my favorite movie *The Shawshank Redemption*

6. You aren't the only one who suffers, for the most part. Not doing anything is not worth it.

7. Living life in fear is not a life well lived. Fear of loving, fear of excitement, and fear of being vulnerable are just that; fears. Choose freedom; especially freedom from the fear of failure. There is a high chance you will get what you want. Try!

8. The contentment that comes with trying to make a change is priceless. It is the journey toward those changes that feels so fulfilling, that the focus on the destination is not an obsessive but loving one.

9. To be in a space where what you think, what you do and what you say are all aligned, is a space of contentment and authenticity. It is beautiful. Dare to experience it.

10. You deserve a more fulfilling, content and peaceful life. Take a step to go get it!

"Change is painful, but nothing is as painful as staying stuck where you don't belong."

— **Mandy Hale**

Thank you for going on this journey with me.

I want to thank you from the bottom of my heart for walking with me and allowing me to share this information with you. I hope you have gotten something out of this commitment to self-growth. It may be your first of many steps. Please reach out to continue pursuing this very important goal of healing and thriving. Remember, what you focus on; grows!

Cheering for your growth, healing and strengthening

Fondly

Sheeza

PS: Please remember to write a review or email me feedback at sheezacounselor@gmail.com. It is so appreciated.

Resources

Beck, Aaron – pioneering psychiatrist in the field of cognitive distortions; colleague of Dr. David Burns. See:

https://psychcentral.com/lib/15-common-cognitive-distortions/

https://psychologypedia.org/aaron-beck-theory-and-cognitive-behavioral-therapy-cbt/

https://www.simplypsychology.org/cognitive-therapy.html

Boss, Pauline – noted American psychotherapist and developer of the theory of ambiguous loss. See:

https://www.ambiguousloss.com/

https://www.psychologytoday.com/us/blog/understanding-grief/201709/ambiguous-loss

Bowlby, John – noted British psychologist and therapist who worked on child development and attachment issues. See:

https://www.simplypsychology.org/bowlby.html

https://healthresearchfunding.org/john-bowlbys-attachment-theory-explained/

Brown, Brene – University of Houston professor of social work who researches shame, vulnerability, and empathy. See:

https://brenebrown.com/

https://brenebrown.com/articles-and-podcasts-with-brene/

Burns, David - pioneering American psychiatrist in the field of cognitive distortions; colleague of Dr. Aaron Beck. See:

https://feelinggood.com/2014/01/06/secrets-of-self-esteem-2-negative-and-positive-distortions/

https://positivepsychology.com/cognitive-distortions/

Cloud, Henry - American spiritual author and psychologist working on the topic of boundaries with John Townsend. See:

https://www.drcloud.com/

https://www.boundaries.me/blog

Covey, Stephen – American businessman and inspirational speaker known for his time and organizational management self-help books. See:

http://stephencovey.comhttps://www.famousauthors.org/stephen-r-covey

DiClemente, Carlo - American health psychologist who developed a model of human behavior change called the Trans theoretical Model, or the Stages of Change

https://www.researchgate.net/profile/Carlo_Diclemente

https://psychcentral.com/lib/stages-of-change/https://exploringyourmind.com/prochaska-diclementes-transtheoretical-model-of-change/

Drucker, Peter – Austrian-American management expert who originated SMART™ goals as part of a program management methodology. See:

https://www.projectsmart.co.uk/brief-history-of-smart-goals.php

https://www.azquotes.com/author/4147-Peter_Drucker

Gottman, John – The Gottman Institute has done intense clinical research on marriage and parenting. See:

www.gottman.com

Johnson, Sue – Canadian clinical psychologist and expert on emotionally-focused couples' therapy. See:

https://www.psychotherapy.net/article/couples/couples-therapy-attachment

http://drsuejohnson.com/

Karpman, Stephen – American psychiatrist who developed the Karpman drama triangle model to explain inter-relationship dynamics in conflict situations. See:

https://www.karpmandramatriangle.com/pdf/202worldpeaceconfpaper.pdf

https://themindsjournal.com/understanding-karpman-drama-triangle/

Perel, Esther - noted Belgian psychotherapist who studies the conflicts between freedom and security in human relationships. See:

https://www.estherperel.com/

https://www.ted.com/speakers/esther_perel

Prochaska, James – American health psychologist who developed a model of human behavior change called the Trans-theoretical Model, or the Stages of Change. See:

https://jprochaska.com/about/james-prochaska/

https://exploringyourmind.com/prochaska-diclementes-transtheoretical-model-of-change/

Shapiro, Francine – an American psychologist and educator who originated, and developed, eye movement desensitization and reprocessing, a form of psychotherapy for resolving the symptoms of traumatic and disturbing life experiences. See:

www.emdr.com

Seligman, Martin – American psychologist who pioneered work on the behavior known as learned helplessness. See:

https://positivepsychology.com/who-is-martin-seligman/

https://www.pursuit-of-happiness.org/history-of-happiness/martin-seligman-psychology/

Townsend, John – American psychologist working on the topic of boundaries. See:

https://www.boundaries.me/blog

https://www.cloudtownsend.com/what-do-you-mean-boundaries-by-dr-henry-cloud-and-dr-john-townsend/

Glossary

Ambiguous loss – the type of loss that occurs when a loved one is physically present in your life, but not emotionally present with you

Amygdala – the section at the bottom of the human brain that is involved in generating a fear response to any type of threat

Anxious-avoidant attachment style – an insecure form of childhood attachment which develops when the mother figure was not a consistent or reliable caregiver for whatever reason

Attachment figures – those persons in your childhood who made you feel loved and cared for

Attachment theory – the theory that the close emotional bond formed between children and their caregivers is what is responsible for laying the foundation for the future bond that develops between adults (in their emotional or romantic relationships)

Bi-cultural identity – the phenomenon of belonging to two different cultures, such as living in one country and having roots or family ties in another

Boundary – limits in a person's emotional, physical, or mental "space" that help define where that person's unique sense of self ends and where another's sense of self begins

Codependence – an unhealthy condition in which one person has too much emotional and/or psychological dependence on a partner or other family member. This partner is needed to an excessive degree in order to meet all of the first person's needs for emotional support and self-esteem.

Collective culture – a type of culture in which the needs of the larger group are thought to be more important than the needs of the individual

Cognitive distortion – an inaccurate, irrational, negative thought about a situation which people tend to cling to as a way to make sense of reality

Cultural competence – the ability to function effectively in any culture that a person must navigate

Desi – an informal term indicating someone or something of Indian, Pakistani, or Bangladeshi origin that (or who) is found abroad

Followership – the tendency to take a follower's position; in other words, a non-dominant position

Genogram – a detailed visual representation or diagram of a family tree, used in psychology to delineate various characteristics that family members share in common

Glorifying – the process of exaggerating the positive features of the recollection one has of past or current events

Gurdwara – a Sikh temple

Individualistic culture – a culture which tends to emphasize the rights and privileges of the individual over those of the family, community, or other collective group

Intergenerational transference – the process of transferring mental or emotional thoughts, feelings, pain, patterns of behavior, and/or problems from one generation to the other

Karpman's drama triangle – a model of negative human social interaction developed by Dr. Stephen Karpman; it describes the various roles of persons involved in an interpersonal conflict

Learned helplessness – a behavior learned by humans and animals who have been subjected to repeated negative experiences, in which the subject comes to believe that there is no remedy for their situation, and therefore stops trying to make the situation better

Limbic system – a set of structures found deep inside the brain that work together to regulate emotions, learning, memory, and sex drive, among other things

Minimizing – the process of downplaying one's memory of an event in the past or the present

Model minority - a demographic group that is commonly believed to be more highly achieving than most of the general population

Paraai – cultural value or construct which holds that a wife "belongs" to her husband and his family

Pareto principle (aka. the 80/20 rule) - the business management principle that states that in a system or process, 20% of the causes will generate 80% of the effects.

Pre-frontal cortex – part of the front of the human brain that controls rational thought and action, including planning and evaluating risks and consequences

Relational boundary – a personal/emotional boundary having to do with close personal relationships

SMART goals™ - goals developed as part of a program management methodology by management expert Peter Drucker. The acronym SMART™ is a mnemonic that stands for the five criteria for a highly effective goal: Specific, Measureable, Actionable, Realistic, and Time-Constrained.

Socioeconomic status (SES) – a measure of a person or family's combined social and economic status calculated using key indicators such as employment, education, home ownership, and financial wealth

Tahiri – aka. tehri, a spicy yellow rice cooked with potatoes, other vegetables, and saffron

Transaction – a psychological term for an interaction between people in which something is exchanged; the exchanged item may be either tangible or intangible

Urgency addiction – a term coined by Stephen Covey for a destructive behavior in which a person procrastinates on completing a larger task by instead completing multiple smaller tasks; this is done to subconsciously impart a feeling of urgency to the larger task, so that the energy associated with that urgency can be harnessed to increase productivity

Wellness wheel – a wheel-shaped model that visually displays the 7 dimensions of wellness: physical, emotional, social, environmental, financial, spiritual, and intellectual

About The Author

Photo Credits - Farah Janjua Photography

A highly trained expert in work and life relationships, Dr. Sheeza Mohsin was born and raised in Karachi, Pakistan, to Indian and Bangladeshi parents. Her dual career involves being a marriage and family therapist/Counselor as well as an Executive Coach. She has worked with hundreds of clients across the globe where she shares her work/life perspective to help her clients in a manner that they can apply what they learn in both settings. Having spent half of her life in South Asia and the other half in America, she brings a unique perspective to understanding the struggle that South Asians in living their emotional and cultural lives, as well as the internal conflict that exists when a person is raised in a conservative background but grows up relatively liberal.

As a multicultural counselor and therapist, Sheeza is sought out by clients dealing with marriage issues, relationship conflicts, and adult and adolescent mental illness, especially in South Asian families. She supports clients in the U.S., Canada, Europe, and Asia. Sheeza has offered family and couples' intensive workshops or a number of years. As a leadership development expert she supports C-suite Leaders strengthen their talent pool and succession. Creating and supporting a work environment that is inclusive and diverse is a strength Sheeza promotes in companies.

Sheeza enjoys travel for work several times a year. She is sought out as a public speaker and consultant by organizations and educational institutions in order to train and educate leaders on various topics. When leading workshops and events, her warm and casual demeanor, sense of humor, along with the ability to engage and connect with people stand out the most. Sheeza regularly volunteers time to board-service for her city, community, and school district. She also participates in diversity-strengthening and peace-oriented movements.

Sheeza completed a Bachelor's degree in business from New York University's prestigious Stern School of Business. She holds a Master's degree in Human Resources Management from Florida International University. Sheeza also earned a PhD from the department of Family Sciences at Texas Women's University. Her specialized training in Leadership Development Models, Clinical topics and Change Management equip her to hit the ground running with clients and companies alike.

Sheeza lives with her two children and dog in a suburb near the Dallas-Fort Worth metroplex. She loves hosting, entertaining and traveling whenever she has the opportunity. Spending time with her kids and family is by far her favorite thing to do.

Sheeza can be contacted at sheezacounselor@gmail.com or by visiting www.sheezamohsin.com for appointment requests and inquiries.

Made in the USA
Coppell, TX
02 March 2020